Filming
TV News
and
Documen-
taries

Filming TV News and Documen- taries

BY JIM ATKINS, JR. AND LEO WILLETTE

CHILTON BOOKS   PHILADELPHIA

A Division of Chilton Company, Publishers

AMPHOTO   NEW YORK

American Photographic Book Publishing Co., Inc.

FOREWORD

A few years ago, when Leo Willette arrived on a commercial airliner in Miami, he was greeted by an ambulance, complete with uniformed attendants and a strait jacket. Willette was rushed from the plane in the restraining jacket and transported by police escort to a plush oceanfront hotel. There a red carpet had been rolled out, and the hotel band was arranged on the steps to greet him. Newsfilm cameras recorded the scene at the airport and at the hotel. It was all a bit of a stunt arranged by a few of Leo's friends, to surprise him.

Leo Willette's entry onto a scene is not always this grandiose. But his entrance has never been quiet or without a touch of controversy.

This book is not quiet, and it will stir some controversy.

In it, Willette and Jim Atkins take a broad look at the state of television newsfilm today. The authors draw heavily on their own experience in the news media. But the book is based in large part on contributions made by some 200 working television news people, who are liberally quoted.

This volume is a start in filling a huge void. As a reference for the student of television news, it should open many avenues of thought. It contains specific tips, from how to shoot aerials, to how to cover a missile launching. And it makes a strong argument for more intelligent use of pictures . . . in this case, well-planned, well-photographed television newsfilm. . . .

Veteran still photographer Joseph Costa, who was a founder of the National Press Photographers Association, has said that "A picture carries with it the presumption of truth."

The most recent Roper survey shows that more people turn to television as their prime source of news than to any other medium. Roper also reports that people *believe* what they see on television more than they believe information they obtain from any other medium.

Hence, television news people have a special responsibility to be sure that their newsfilm is informative, is interesting, and tells the truth.

Willette and Atkins have taken a big step forward in spreading the word on the potential of well-planned, well-executed newsfilm material. There will be controversy about some of the methodology in the book and some of the author's conclusions.

But the book will be read. And as it is read, it will arouse students, working newsfilm photographers and editors, television news directors and station management. In this way it will prove most valuable.

Detroit, Michigan

HOWARD BACK
Executive Editor,
National Television News

CONTENTS

Chapter 1

WHAT IS NEWS

Of the countless hours of television programming each year, none should offer more impact, appeal, and vitality than that small percentage of air-time devoted to news. The key word, however, is "should." It is a regretable fact that in too many communities and markets, television news lacks not only audience appeal and vitality, but is, in fact, dull, unimaginative, predictable, and easily forgettable.

Need news be the object of audience ho-hummism? Of course not. News is as vital and dynamic as the day by day story of how you, your family, and your neighbors are living right now — along with an insight into the promises of tomorrow. News, then, is you!

Especially on the local level, news is the link which binds a community. News is that new section of super highway, the one which will cut five minutes each way as you drive to and from work. News is the contract for a junior high which will be completed and open just in time to absorb your growing children.

News can be that blind intersection four blocks away — the one which has claimed three lives in the past half year (about time we pressure City Hall for that traffic light).

News is a hunk of history, perhaps in the form of the old "haunted house" of your childhood — to be torn down to make space for a new fire station. News can be the burning dump which might be the cause of your asthma; or new research at the medical center in Central City — research which could lead to a longer, fuller life for you. News can be the reminder that traffic police are stepping-up their campaign against speeders. News is a plan for those pesky drainage ditches and their overflow during heavy rains.

It is the fire in that house across town — the fire caused by overloaded electrical circuits. ("Say, that house was about the same age as mine. Is it possible my circuits. . . .")

It is a zoning modification which almost slipped through City Hall unnoticed — one which would have plunked a low-rent housing scheme right in the middle of a suburban neighborhood that boasts neatness, pride of ownership, and mortgages to prove it.

News is . . .

News is all this. And more. Yet, as we noted, some TV news productions lack the punch and persuasion to get this across. Why? Well, before we see what television news may not always be — let us first examine what it is.

Television news is potentially the most dynamic and personal form of communication in the evolution of man. With it, on a day-by-day basis, the achievements, the weaknesses, the sins and the strengths of mankind can be recorded, then reported. A television report can use words, natural sounds, movement, a picture which can freeze an instant for eternity — and motion pictures; newsfilm which transforms the casual viewer into a captivated onlooker.

Although the writers and reporters are often loath to admit this, it is the camerawork, motion picture film, and edited newsfilm which give television this characteristic of personalized mass communication. In the minds of many, the sinew and strength of electronic reporting is newsfilm.

A story is a story. But with newsfilm, the same story is an experience; a living animated event the viewer shares with the newsfilm reporter. Newsfilm makes your viewer an eyewitness to the news. It is a fresh, provocative, challenging approach to journalism, bursting with impact and realism.

Newsmen on Film

Ernie Schultz, News Director, WKY-TV, Oklahoma City, says:

"News and weather have always been the backbone of local programming at WKY-TV. The emphasis was set by the time the station was programming full time.

"At various times, we have experimented in TV news with lots of gimmicks. We even had a full-time artist in the news department at one time, to help with graphics and animation.

"But, as we learned more about what television can do for news, we became more and more convinced that newsfilm was the area in which to concentrate our money and manpower. We use our live cameras to cover the legislature, the president's visit, the city council debates; but film, and the control it permits, is the mainstay of our news operation.

"We feel that newsfilm is basically what makes TV a better news medium than any other. It isn't the reporting — the newspapers have more and maybe better reporters. It isn't necessarily the airmen. One of the best in town is on radio. But, neither the newspaper nor radio can *show* you the news, as it happened, the way it happened. And we work hard to do just that with film. We have had some famous alumni from among our newscasters — Frank McGee, Bob Gamble and Dick John, to name just a few. But our news film cameramen are just as illustrious in their fields; men like Scott Berner and Houston Hall.

"All members of the TV news staff are photographers, and all take pride in good film, well-shot and well-edited. We are all students of cinematography, the rules of reference line, sequence, and matched action. We don't always follow all the rules, but we always try.

"This reliance upon newsfilm can be trying at times. Sixteen mm equipment used by all TV newsmen is about twenty years out of date by 8mm standards. There is still the chance that because only one of a hundred possible mistakes was made, the film will not be usable. There is always the concern when you edit an hour-long hearing on a controversial new law to two minutes that you haven't been fair to each side. It is sometimes difficult to impress upon the new electronic journalist, fresh from college, the importance of knowing how to run a camera, a splicer and a Houston machine. He'd much rather be on the air, doing a poor imitation of David Brinkley."

Deacon Anderson, News Director, KPIX, San Francisco, says:

"A good TV news program is one that informs in a memorable fashion. It has to inform. It has to be memorable. This means, among other things, that it has to be chock-full of *good* film. The thing that makes a news story memorable is the quality of film.

"We have five photographers at KPIX News. Once a week we have a conference to discuss technique, equipment, new standards, ethics, quality control — the whole gamut of newsfilm. There are thousands of television cameramen in this business, but a photographer in the whole sense of the word is as rare as snow in San Diego. A photographer is not a man who squirts film past a lens while aiming his camera at something that moves. A photographer is a sensitive being, one who understands the emotional values of creative lighting, who uses expansion and compaction as a creative tool to interpret the spirit of an event, who knows the very limits of technique so that he can go those limits when the situation demands it. He is in no way a hack.

"On a given day, cameramen from four to seven stations will be assigned to cover an event. More often than not most of the filmwork is much the same on the air. But if one of those cameramen is a photographer, the difference between his work and that of the others is *instantly* noticed.

"Exposure, focus, depth of field, cutaways, length of segments, establishing shots, close-ups — these things are common to all cameramen. But these things are a palette to a photographer.

"The difference between a cameraman and a photographer is the difference between a cliché and a well-turned phrase. The 'stand up and shoot the subject' is as out of mode as rip-and-read. Beyond anything else, the crying need of television news today is for good photographers who are masters of the trade and can work quickly.

"The difference between TV film men and others is that we are governed by circumstance, rather than governing circumstance. We don't control where things will happen nor when, nor the order of the event, nor the time it will take from beginning to end. So our people have to be razor sharp to walk into a generally unfamiliar circumstance and walk out a few minutes later with interpretive film. On the rare occasion when there is time, he should come back with film which is superb.

"Is there a future in TV local news? You bet your life there is! The three network stations in San Francisco program more than sixteen hours of local news a week, and this will jump to twenty hours. People are more anxious to see what's going on than to read about it, or even hear about it. They don't want to be told the Mayor let loose a blast at the City Attorney today, they want to watch the Mayor's tirade. Only television news allows them to do that.

"The recent California floods illustrate that. We had crews all over Northern California and we had fresh film of the disaster several times a day, some of it taken three hours before air time more than 300 miles away."

Why, Oh Why?

Now, if all of this is so, why do so many local television news programs feature rather anemic film stories?

To begin with, most of us prefer to work with the tools with which we are most familiar. And since most television news directors and executives graduate through the ranks of newspaper reporting and television writing, they naturally favor the words. (Some, we note sadly, unconsciously look upon film as a necessary evil.) The somewhat sobering truth is this: After talking and dealing with hundreds of TV newsmen, news directors, news writers, and the like; after attending dozens of conventions, seminars, and briefings, your authors are uncomfortably convinced that the men who run many television news departments simply do not know enough about the photographic tools of their trade. Many news executives and station managers have no idea what a camera can do and what it cannot do. Far too many fail to recognize or reward creative filming and techniques — seemingly preferring the hackneyed and unoriginal.

Too Many Words

Rather than learn about film and what goes into producing good newsfilm, too many of them will go topheavy on words; either ignoring film or accepting it on an "anything goes" basis. And when the department or station leaders do not care, this indifference filters down into the attitudes and performances of a staff.

For the neophyte cameraman *really* intending to learn his profession, there is nothing more rewarding than joining the staff of a tough, uncompromising, no-nonsense news director who knows what is best in newsfilm, who demands creativity and imagination under even the most routine situations, and who will settle for nothing less than 100 per cent professionalism.

It is the purpose of this book to provide for the student, cameraman, news director, newsfilm editor, documentary producer, and television executive a platform of fact, opinion, experience, and example toward effective newsfilm, and to examine the techniques of editing and presentation that make a TV screen pulsate with immediacy and impact.

Chapter 2

EQUIPMENT

Every photographer has his own favorite photographic equipment. But a camera that is light doesn't have the extras needed on a particular job; the small sound camera doesn't hold enough film. No one camera meets all of the newsman's requirements.

It's the same with films. Du Pont 930 and 931 Reversal films are standard at WBRC-TV, Birmingham. WTOP-TV, Washington, D. C., uses Du Pont 936 and 937 negative films for the most part. Many photographers prefer Kodak Tri-X or Plus-X. Films are a compromise too. Sometimes you need a fast film, but the slow films give better quality.

For the beginning cameraman or reporter-photographer who has other duties, we recommend that you get one simple camera, maybe a Bell & Howell 16mm DL-70, and use one fast film. You won't make as many mistakes. Learn to use this camera, to load it automatically, to estimate the exposure for the particular film you've chosen. In other words, make it simple. When you learn to use this camera and this one film expertly, begin experimenting with another camera and films.

How One Station Operates

Hal Saylor, WTOP-TV, Washington, D. C., photographer, says he uses Du Pont 936 negative film for the most part. This is a fast film with an ASA rating of 250.

"I use an 8N5 filter outdoors," he says. "This cuts the exposure down 2½ stops. We use negative because we can process it faster. Also, when you shoot negative film, you have more latitude."

He uses a Bell & Howell 100-foot hand camera because it is almost indestructible, and for sound he uses an Auricon Super 1200 with a zoom lens.

He keeps his equipment in four cases, always ready to go. Each box weighs 50 pounds, so one man can handle them.

WTOP-TV photographers shoot about 2000 feet of film a day. They can process the first 100 feet of film in fifteen minutes, and can run additional film through at 50 feet a minute.

Cameras

Movie cameras are now being produced that are relatively automatic. The cameras most used by television newsmen are the 16mm Bell & Howell and the Bolex. Both hold 100 feet of film.

The Bolex H-16 Rex 3 can do more tricks than the B & H and has superior viewing, including reflex viewing. It has filter slots, automatic threading, and a footage counter which returns to zero automatically. It weighs six pounds and is easy to handle.

Bell & Howell 70DR, 16mm spool-loading camera.

Bell & Howell 70HR, 16mm spool-loading camera.

The Bolex Automatic 16mm zoom camera is a single lens camera which features viewing through a removable Preview finder mounted on the side of the camera. It is the newest silent camera in the 16mm field. It features a reflex viewing and focusing system that permits focusing with diaphragm fully opened. It sets the lens opening automatically, but the diaphragm can be controlled manually. "This camera," says NBC News Photographer Robin Still, "is the camera of the future. I was amazed at how quickly it changes [lens opening automatically], and how good it is."

The Bell & Howell is cheaper than the Bolex and has no frills. It is sturdy and easy to operate. You can jump up and down on it and then take film. The group-coupled lens and viewfinder turrets automatically position the viewfinder and lens, which is a blessing when you are rushed. A photographer should learn to use both of these cameras.

The Arriflex is the finest 16mm on the market, but it is out of price range for most local news operations. It costs over $1800 without magazines. Robin Still says, "It's the finest camera made for news or documentary filming."

The Arriflex is the most expensive movie camera used in news coverage. Here Mike O'Connor, WWL-TV, New Orleans, uses one outside Trinity College, Dublin.

This is the Auricon Pro-600, in use by many television newsrooms.

The Auricon Pro-600 Special can be modified to use magnetic sound.

The Auricon Cine-Voice, 100-foot sound camera, is the workhorse of most news departments. The camera is light, and can be modified for larger magazines. A transistor sound amplifier also can be used.

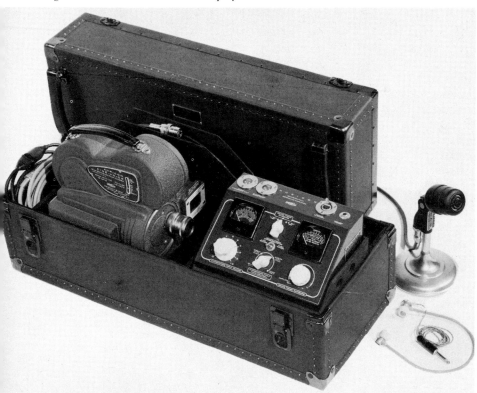

The Sound Camera

The Auricon Cine-Voice II 16mm sound-on-film camera is the camera used by many television news operations. It will hold only 100 feet of film, but most stations modify the camera to take larger magazines, and the result is a sound camera that can be hand held.

The Auricon Pro-600 is also popular with TV news operations. It holds 600-foot magazines. A tripod is needed to operate this camera.

New Portable Sound

Beckman & Whitley (San Francisco), has developed a 16mm sound-on-film camera for ABC News that weighs fourteen pounds with lens and loaded magazine. This camera — the CM 16 — will hold a 400-foot or 1200-foot magazine. It is equipped with a zoom lens and records magnetic sound. The magazine is attached to the back of the camera, which balances on the photographer's shoulder. This allows him to sight a full horizon.

Jack Bush, Director of Newsfilm for ABC News, calls it "a major breakthrough" in the search for a real portable 16mm sound camera. Bush says this camera allows the cameraman to concentrate on the action. He adds that the camera requires less power and can operate under difficult conditions, such as extreme cold. Up to thirty minutes of film can be shot in a single run. This camera makes most other 16mm news sound cameras obsolete.

Reality and portability are two more ingredients of the future, for reality and a sense of being present more than outweigh a certain amount of camera-shakiness.

A Sound-Film System

The Eastman Kodak Company has developed a complete 16mm film-recording and playback system for television. This includes: (1) single-system camera, the Kodak Reflex Special Camera; (2) negative and positive 16mm films; (3) a really automatic, rapid-processing machine; and (4) a 16mm television projector.

The processor takes up only three square feet. It has other advantages — including a unique one-time-use chemical system. Negative film can be developed at a rate of eighteen feet per minute.

This complete system has many advantages: one Kodak consultant can give you full details on the entire system; one man can service your equipment; you go to only one office for information; and the technology of film and equipment is developed for compatibility. The development processor operates with push-button consistency, and it takes only 60 seconds lead time. The camera is not designed for news work, although it can do the job. For a station that is beginning with only one camera and a small amount of equipment, this system is worth looking into. The camera is versatile, and although it is not

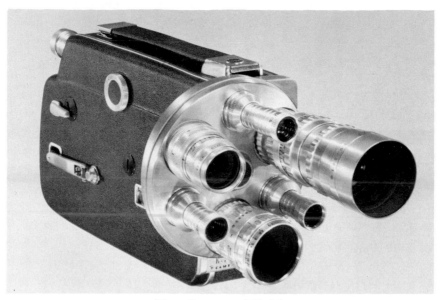

Photo Courtesy of Kodak

The Cine-Kodak K-100 Turret Camera is used by many newsmen. Special advantage is its 40-foot run in a single running.

The Kodak Reflex Special Camera provides a complete 16mm motion-picture system for both silent film and for recording magnetic sound. It has a reflex viewing system for easy focusing.

the answer to a news photographer's dream, it can do any job in television, from shooting a sound interview to filming a silent commercial.

Fast Processor

Fairchild has manufactured a "Mini-Rapid" processor, Model F-316a, that sells for around $1,500, which is portable, small, and fast. It processes 16mm film at six feet per minute, and features leaderless delivery. You can look at the first feet in a few minutes and change development time if it is not exposed properly. It requires no plumbing, so can be used anywhere. It can process film strips from as short as two feet to 400 feet with one chemical loading. It weighs only 65 pounds.

A Compromise

Remember this about 16mm camera equipment: every camera is a compromise. While one offers refinements, such as devices for dissolves, it may lack a certain ruggedness. Another offers through-the-lens focusing, but is large and bulky. A third camera offers other advantages but bucks like a bronco on the first few frames when not anchored down on a tripod.

Bob Gamble of Indianapolis, Indiana, thinks often of the future of local television news. Gamble, News Manager of WFBM, thinks techniques and equipment should undergo dramatic improvements. "By and large," he says, "the sound cameras used today are those developed for amateur photographers fifteen to twenty years ago — with some refinement.

"It is possible for a television cameraman to have a reasonably small camera, weighing about twenty pounds, that contains its own power supply, its own light, and its own wireless microphone. [Then] ... television journalism will have a dimension — to transmit news events — not simply to recreate."

What About 8mm?

Cameramen used to think it was impossible to shoot news with anything but a 35mm camera. Now, 16mm cameras are used almost exclusively, and the 8mm camera is being tested for use in news.

Dick Hance, Executive Producer, WGN-TV News, Chicago, believes that in a few years the 8mm will be the camera used by most local television news departments. The cost of 8mm film and equipment is much lower. It is estimated that film and processing costs are cut 60 per cent by the use of 8mm, from 16mm costs. Hance says that 8mm can be adapted to TV newsfilm as the equipment becomes better and that the sound quality from the 8mm magnetic stripe is as good as single-system optical 16mm track.

Charles Carter, chief engineer for WESH-TV, Orlando, Florida, believes that in the future his station will be able to reproduce 8mm pictures that are as good as 16mm.

The Fairchild 8mm Zoom Sound Camera has been used by many TV news-men. The authors believe that television stations will soon be using 8mm cameras.

CHAN-TV photographer uses the Fairchild 8mm Zoom Sound Camera to film an interview. CHAN-TV, Vancouver, B.C., uses 8mm sound-on-film and finds the quality good.

R. G. Hennessey, general manager of Fairchild's Industrial Products Division, is shown with the "TV Sound Movie Package," which includes a Fairchild 8mm sound movie camera and sound projector plus a Fairchild "Mini-Rapid" 16mm film processor for quick processing of black and white newsfilm.

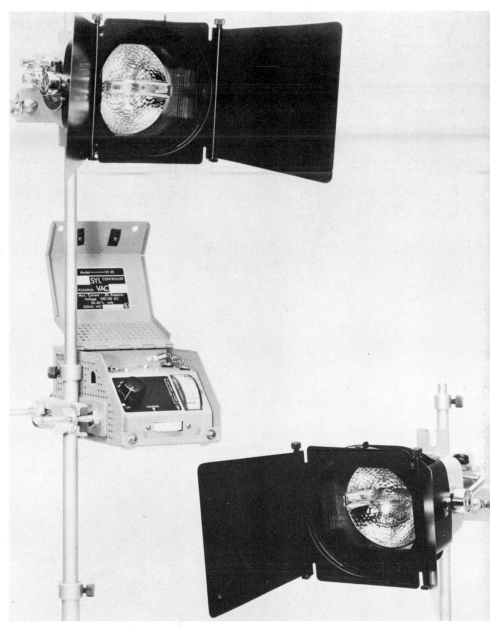

The Professional Photo Light by Sylvania is a studio light that is easy to move for use on location. The Sylvac Control, Model SV-9, provides control of light intensity and color balance.

25

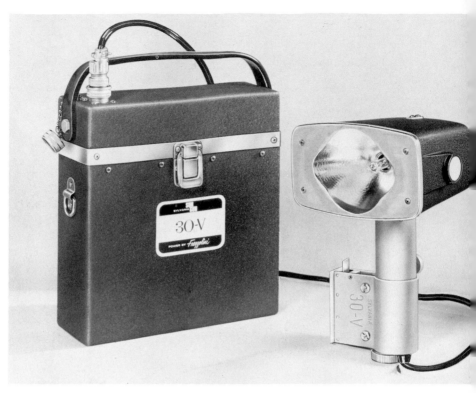

Photo Courtesy Sylvania

The problems of a portable light source have been served. The Sylvania Sun Gun Movie Light goes anywhere.

This is the Sylvania 30-V with fingertip variable beam control. The portable power pack can be recharged in one hour.

In addition, because of improved developers and sound recording techniques, it is safe to say that 8mm can be used to obtain today's 16mm quality. At this writing Fairchild is field-testing a professional 8mm sound movie camera aimed towards the television news market.

Everyone agrees that since 8mm is cheaper and easier to handle than 16mm, it will be used in television news; it's just a matter of when.

Lighting

With new fast films, most newsfilm can be shot with existing light. Certain lights are, however, useful. There are many, but the Sylvania Sun Gun series offers a wide variety, including portable lights suitable for studio illumination.

The Battery-Powered Sun Gun 30-V, with a variable beam that can be focused, can handle most news-gathering chores. The battery pack can be recharged in one-hour. The Sun Gun II is an excellent light which is powered by electric current.

Time and Care

When spare time does come along, the cameraman should welcome and use the extra minutes. Projectors can be cleaned, cameras can be oiled, the editing table can be straightened out, splicers can be cleaned with solvents (never, never use razor blades).

WWL-TV, New Orleans, assignment reporter Henry Teles notes the pet newsroom peeve of many non-cameramen — the fact that many lensmen fritter away their time between assignments.

"Some wait until a hot story breaks before they decide the gas is low in the newscar," Teles says, "or before they notice that they haven't loaded the camera since taking out their last filmed assignment."

Behind the Camera

John M. Cooper, manager of newsfilm, CBS News, said that the future of television newsfilm is tied up with satellites, which make it possible to transmit newsfilm across the Atlantic on a regular basis.

"Along with electronic distribution of newsfilm, we may expect continuing improvements in cameras and film," says Cooper. "Some of these may provide quality advances as dramatic as the switch, a few years ago, from optical to magnetic sound track. But the great need will always be competent cameramen. There are too few of these."

Chapter 3

THE NEWSROOM

How the old newsrooms have changed! It seems like fifty years ago that the authors left the heady confines of newspaper city rooms for the lonely, quiet, and mystifying newsroom of television. In truth, though, it has been a mere ten years, but what a decade of progress.

It was different then, when the pangs of conscience (or the FCC, more likely) began to gnaw at station managers — when they awakened to the fact that news can be more than rip-and-read, presented by an announcer.

Today, even the smallest TV newsrooms will boast fine tripods, portable lights and sound equipment, a newscar or two, some two-way and police radios, two pairs of geared re-winds, a fine projector, SOF (sound on film) or magnetic sound equipment, a secretary, and a boss who won't make you spool your own daylight reels from 1200 feet of raw stock.

How It Works

How does a modern newsroom operate? At WTVJ, Miami, editor and assignment man Tony Kucherak was seated like a slot-man at a newspaper. Around him were the desks for reporter-cameramen; overhead, two or three different radios — police, metro police, and Dade County sheriff's radio — if memory serves. There was an executive office for News Director Ralph Renick, and the management treated their news director in an executive manner. Renick was not tied down editing newsfilm or handling the myriad of trifling details that go into the newsroom's operation.

Rather, Renick could *think*, unharrassed by the blasting phone, unhurried by impatient management. From these precincts, Renick was to produce some of the first and most memorable triumphs of local television.

Name some of the ingredients of TV news which make one proud today, and chances are Renick and WTVJ were first — first local daily editorial

A newsroom in the old days was often no more than a desk and some phones. Now, a newsroom is filled with the best editing and news-gathering equipment available.

Ralph Renick, vice president in charge of news, WTVJ-TV, Miami, Florida, is shown in his modern office.

(emphasis on *local:* no chewing out of DeGaulle, but the politician next door
. . . the guy who could hit back) ; first of the excellent locally produced documentaries (see chapter on documentaries) ; first TV news director to bring
real weight, authority, dignity, and responsibility to the profession.

WTVJ News has since moved into its own building, alongside the main
studios and offices. With some 21 people in his news department, Renick and
staff had to design a businesslike office to avoid falling all over each other and
the equipment.

The Design

How should a news department be designed? The newsroom is going to be
what space the station gives you. If you can, always argue for more room. In
the long run more and more members will be added to your staff, and you never
want management to think, "Where did all those guys in that small office
come from?"

It is a far better tactic to have a small staff looking very lonely inside a
large set of offices. Then it looks like the rooms need some filling — with, say,
additional equipment and another cameraman or two. Once the space is committed, start thinking about where things and people should go.

The AP or UPI wires should be sound-proofed in some manner — a former
closet, perhaps, with a glass half-door for peeking and peering. Ditto with the
wirephoto machine; the screeches and cackles which come from it could drive
anyone berserk.

The squawking police radio should be placed as far as possible from the
area where SOF is going to be "viewed" on a projector. And remember, the
person who has to answer the phone the most should also be somewhat removed
from the police radio — though within earshot of picking up important signals.

Naturally, the two-way radio must be near someone's desk — preferably the
same person answering the phones. A good secretary in this corner is often the
answer; while checking down a fire from the police radio and the telephone
with one hand, she can be dispatching a newscar via the two-way radio with
the other.

Keep your editing tables as far from the traffic stream as possible. Your
film editor needs all the concentration he can command. One interruption, sometimes, and the editing of an intricate piece of film has to be started all over.
Near the editor must be a projector. Ideally, the screening surface for this
projector should be within viewing angle of anyone in the news department
who wishes to see it without leaving his desk.

The newsroom should be kept clear of all trivia. Office supplies, old scripts,
the film morgue should be shifted out of sight, out of the room, but close enough
to grab when needed.

To explain the workings of the newspaper slot-man—rim-men arrangement
would take too much space to discuss here; but before the newsroom is laid out,

it would serve the newsman well to get a newspaper reporter or editor over to the nearest cocktail lounge and have him sketch out the workings.

Whether the news operation is large or small, the greatest economy of money and time in figuring out what should go where may be achieved in a rather simple way: find some newsroom which has gone through the headaches, made the mistakes, ironed out the wrinkles, and come up with a good plan. Then visit this newsroom and steal every good idea they have.

What to Carry in Your Car

It takes only one torrential downpour to convince any cameraman who-has-enough-sense-to-come-out-of-the-rain (but can't) that he should include foul-weather gear in his bag of tricks. A "war surplus" store is a natural for this rain gear. Ditto hip-boots for covering floods of various dimensions, and snow-garb for those areas where snow is heavy.

The trunk of any newscar should hold a treasure trove of things that someday, on some story, are not only likely to come in handy, but may make the difference in getting the story, or watching it slip by. In the trunk might go:

Flashlight, with spare batteries and bulb — for the countless times when strange terrain must be navigated in pitch darkness.

Tape measure — for use when a really accurate footage count is needed.

Super-telephoto lens — *i.e.,* 6″ or so. A couple of times a year the best shot available is going to be offered from a distance and at an angle where only

The television news cameraman must be equipped for any emergency situation. Here a newsman covers a hurricane.

a high-powered telephoto lens can take it; usually where closer shots are either physically impossible or where foliage cuts visability to nothing (a plane wreckage on a distant hillside, or inside factory grounds where company guards bar the way).

Changing bag — it's incredible how a camera will jam when there's no closet handy, when the cameraman will have to "go into it," and in cases where he can't expose a single frame of important footage.

Bathing suit — an old one you've decided to discard. Don't. You never can tell.

Lens tissue — a must after covering muddy, rainy, dusty, or icy story locations.

Orange sticks — for cleaning built-up film emulsion from camera.

Camera oil — for the camera you forgot to attend to at home over the past few weeks and which is audibly growling and grinding in protest.

Folding Reflector — a nicety for fill-in when time and patience allows (or pure professionalism demands). Easily constructed in these days of light plywood, cheap hinges, and aluminum foil.

Spare winding key — a certain common hand-held 16mm camera has a remarkably bad tendency toward allowing winding keys to snap off in direct proportion to the cameraman's distance from a replacement.

Small assorted screw drivers — include some Phillip's-head ones.

Tape — of the masking variety. Never, never use cellophane tape around cameras, films, or editing tables; it's too hard to spot, too easy to jam something.

Legal size, lined pad — not only for notes, but for "scripts" where the cameraman might wish to do a location, two-projector piece. Words can be printed with marking pencil, and the pages taped together with masking tape, then rolled alongside the take-lens by any handy volunteer.

Spare cans — all exposed film should be placed in these. So should "split reels," *i.e.*, when cameraman has to change from color to black-and-white, or to faster film.

Spare Daylight Spools — same reasons as above, plus the fact that some take-up reels get bent and can cause film-jams in cameras.

Chapter 4

FINDING NEWS

Gene Fowler, newspaperman and author, wrote in his autobiography, *Skyline:* "News is history shot on the wing. The huntsmen from the Fourth Estate seek to bag only the peacock or the eagle of the swifting day."

Television news is, for the most part, shot on the wing, or at least on the run. While you can interview witnesses or participants after the event is over, the best of TV newsfilm is shot because a news photographer knew how to find news and was there when it happened.

How to be there — that's the problem. Let's look at a day in the life of a newsfilm photographer to get an idea of how to go about finding news.

The first thing a newsman does in the morning (unless he's called out of bed to cover a fire or other catastrophe), is to call his newsroom for messages. Then he switches on the radio to listen to the morning news and find out what has happened since the morning papers went to press. Next, he reads the morning papers for leads and ideas, background and followups. He makes notes and clips the stories he is interested in covering. Later that clip may contain the address he needs, or the name of a contact.

At the newsroom leads are coming in. The wire services, United Press International and Associated Press, will carry stories on what's happening today, as well as a listing of important events and press conferences.

Anyone Is a Source

Anyone is a potential news source. One of your authors was awakened at 3 o'clock one morning by loud banging at the front door. He went to the door to find his milkman standing there, rain-soaked. He was told the area was flooding. The sleepy newsman rushed out of the house in raincoat and pajamas and went to work on what would be that day's top story. You might say Jim Atkins found a story on his own doorstep.

Leave everyone with these words: "Call me if you see a good story." Some of them will. And leave behind a business card with home, office, and mobile phone numbers.

There are a few sources which can consistently supply you with good items. Important people usually arrive by plane. So have several ticket agents as contacts.

The radio operator at the sheriff's office or police department knows more about what's going on around town than any other single source. Make sure he knows you want news tips. And, if possible, take him to lunch once in a while and talk shop. Let him learn what you consider news.

In most news operations, the police radio is the second most vital link in communication — second only to the telephone. From the police radio comes an assortment of clues to what is going on in a community. To the trained, news-conscious cameraman it provides the jagged hunks of a day-by-day community mosaic.

Here is an accident . . . there a stake-out (the Chief's going after the bookies again) . . . an ambulance needed downtown (natural causes, sounds like heart) . . . a fire extinguisher was all that was needed in that small motel fire (another charred mattress bites the dust) . . . car 6 has broken down again (maybe there's a story here; are our police cars getting obsolete or is City Garage maintenance fumbling the ball?) . . . broken windows at Jefferson Elementary School (not the first time, either) . . . another traffic jam on the overpass (or does this cease to be news?) . . . paddy wagon called to 800 block of Lafayette Street (those cheap ginmills are ruining that block — fast) . . . a narcotics suspect (things have been quiet lately; how come?) . . . a prowler suspect at 718 Brunswick (poor Mrs. Henderson and her imagination — this is the third call from her in the past week). . . .

Some news departments think so much of this type of communication with news sources that they keep a bank of short wave radios going simultaneously: police, sheriff's band, fire department, ship-to-shore, and others.

Obviously there are different needs from one market to another. Where in the Far West the newsman might want a radio with which to keep on top of forest fires, the man in a port city might want something else — Coast Guard Search and Rescue, for example.

To the person who has never worked under the constant barrage of beeps and signals which pour from one or more police-type radios, the whole idea sounds impossible: living through such maddening cacophony, actually getting other work done, and learning to train the ear to filter out the routine and react instinctively to the sounds which mean news.

There are a half-dozen or more ways in which the man in the newsroom learns to disregard the noisy and the insignificant. In time he learns to perk up and quickly grab what is essential.

The newsmen in Miami, Florida, are quite lucky. There, the police give an indication right off the bat as to the seriousness of the call, then give details as to what and where. Like this: "Code 3, Car 79 to 4040 Northwest Third, on a 14." The instant the newsman hears "Code 3" he knows it is important. A "Code 1" or "Code 2" probably would drift right by his consciousness. But in Miami, Code 3 means it's big.

Sometimes the car that gets the call is a tip-off to the real nature of the story. Certain cars tend to specialize; burglary teams, narcotic squads, juvenile detectives, etc. The "signal," however, is usually the most clarifying feature to a police call. In the case of the fictitious Miami call, the signal would be the phrase, "on a 14." A "14" in one city might mean armed robbery, in another it might mean a peeping tom. Learning the signals in one's market thus becomes the newsman's first problem in using the police radio.

It seems so basic to say, we are almost reluctant to say it, but we will anyway: every newscar in every news department should be equipped with a police radio. In fact, conscientious newsmen will insist on police radios in every private car within the department.

The reason this bears saying is that in one metropolitan market in a large southern city, the department's only police radio is located in the newsroom. And, incredible as it sounds, each of the three news cars is equipped with regular AM radios; presumably so that reporters and cameramen may be entertained to and from assignments. Doubtless, this is a well entertained news organization. Their competition is not nearly so entertained; but it gets a lot more news and clobbers the "well entertained" department in the ratings.

For the free-lance cameraman, the police radio means dollars. It also means getting that full-time job, if that is what the free-lancer is aiming for.

One free-lancer we know in the East has his entire family geared to listen in to the police radio. He has such radios sprinkled liberally throughout his house — in the kitchen, by the TV set, in the garage, even in the bedroom (which is being more zealous than most care to become).

Although the last time we saw this man's family at work his children were in the toddling stage, there is little doubt that, today, even his six-year old is probably muttering: "Mommy . . . did you catch that signal 38 on Willow Street?"

This free-lancer is so good and makes so much money that he has turned down numerous offers for jobs in the very news departments to whom he sells his film. He can't afford the reduction in income.

What to Look For

Every newsman knows to cover a fire or a murder or a tornado. But big stories are few and far between in most cities. You have to find stories you can illustrate with movie film for the daily news shows. That's where digging comes in. Anything that is of interest or affects a large number of people is news. You must find the largest common denominator. Newspaper readers can look through the pages, skipping stories that don't interest them. In television, each film must be of general interest to your audience, if you want to keep an audience.

If you want to find out what people are thinking about in your city, listen to what they say at breakfast. Eat an early breakfast in a small diner and listen. You can make a quick interest survey by listening to a dozen or so people. They will be discussing the stories that hit home, and these stories call for extra coverage. In the evenings try listening in to conversations at the neighhood taverns.

Lee Hanna, director of Radio News for CBS, says that news should be popular, should be what people talk about. He adds: "What the taxi-cab driver talks about. What people talk about at lunch. Every newscast need not lead with the Cyprus situation. Topless bathing suits are also of news interest."

PR Men and the News

Public Relations men are producers of news. An efficient and honest public relations man, armed with news judgment, can be a real help. He can furnish tips and information and can set up interviews. If he's smart he will call you when he hears a story not connected with his client. One Broadway columnist gives PR men one free plug for every three real news tips they provide him.

Press releases are a fruitful source of news, and Washington newsmen couldn't operate without them; they just couldn't cover it all. Locally, a press release about a new plant, a bank opening, or a press conference can be the beginning of worthwhile and timely newsfilm. Scott Cutlip, University of Wisconsin journalism professor, says: "An ever-increasing share of the news on TV is coming straight from PR men to the public." More than 5,000 releases flood the offices of the financial editors of the New York Herald Tribune and the New York Times each week.

There are some 100,000 public relations men in this country. Too few ever come up with good news items. They will badger you with news and views of movie stars, politicians, labor leaders, charity drives, and dog shows, but if you're in the news business, you'll have to work with them. Each offering from a public relations man must be judged on its merit. If you can develop a film that is newsworthy and interesting from a PR tip, the PR man's client deserves a plug.

Jim Moran, a flack of the old school, has sat on an ostrich egg (and hatched it) to publicize the movie, "The Egg And I." He has pulled all sorts of stunts and has made himself more famous than any of his clients. Still, he does a service for his clients and for the press.

In just about any town other than New York City, you'll know many of the PR men you deal with personally, and you'll know which ones you can work with and the few you can't.

Many newsmen have less than kind words to say about public relations practitioners and press agents. Dick Schaap, columnist for the New York Herald Tribune, says: "A good percentage of them are utterly worthless. Their main function is to get in the way of stories. They tell so many lies about their clients that even the clients begin to believe them. There are dozens of Hollywood stars who actually believe that they once were prize fighters. The best policy, in almost all cases, is to avoid press agents, or at least distrust them."

One New York newspaper sends out a memo to all reporters and editors informing the staff of any unethical operations of PR men. But a public relations man can be a big help to the news photographer if he will offer ideas for news stories and help the photographer get the story. He must be accessible. A bad public relations man gets bad coverage for his clients. He must cooperate with the photographer and make it easier, not harder, to get the story. Educate the PR men to serve TV news as well as the newspapers.

The press and magazines are full of stories of PR men and their unsuccessful attempts to influence newsmen. What the PR profession needs is a good public relations program.

The Competition

Read the newspapers and news magazines. Look at the TV news shows on competing channels and listen to the radio. News may come from any of these sources. You may read in "Newsweek" that the governor of your state is planning to run for the Senate. Almost embarrassing, perhaps, but it happens.

You must keep a close watch on the competition to make sure that you are not covering stories they have already fully covered. Almost anything a newspaper can cover, television can cover. Television stations now editorialize. If your station does editorialize, use films to illustrate editorials. The result will be more impact, and a more interesting package.

In New York City, WOR-TV, WNBC-TV and WCBS-TV are reviewing plays. John Wingate, WOR-TV; Lee Jordan, WCBS-TV, and Leonard Probst, WNBC-TV, are now rushing to their respective studios after the curtain drops on Broadway. They have their reviews on the air by 11 p.m. Wingate says: "A quick synopsis of a play can tell as much as a newspaper review and has the advantage of being briefer." Any local station can offer reviews of plays and movies. Use film of a rehearsal, or an interview with a performer or producer. You can also use publicity stills for visuals with reviews of films or plays.

The Power Elite

In every city there are politicians, public officials, businessmen, philanthropists, civic leaders, industrialists, officials of organizations, chiefs of police, attorneys, and others who run things. When something happens in your town, members of the power elite will be involved. Get to know the power elite. It is your best source of news.

Most important news comes about because somebody important is doing something important. T. S. Eliot wrote: "Most of the trouble in the world is caused by people wanting to be important." What they do to become important is news.

The Politicians

Politicians are a major source of news. In *The Fourth Branch of Government*, Douglass Cater (former Washington editor of *The Reporter*, and now an assistant to President Johnson), says: "The member of Congress is uniquely a creature and creator of publicity."

Politics is conflict. It is war without guns. And every political race is a long-running story. What your city council does, what your state legislature does, what your governor does, or doesn't do, is always news.

Build up your contacts in political circles. Gain the confidence of someone in the inner circle. He can give you leads and keep you up-to-date on the local political situation and that all-important background.

It is the duty of the television newsman to cover this story. LeRoy Collins, former president of the National Association of Broadcasters, and now Director of the Federal Community Relations Service, told the 42nd Annual Convention of the NAB: "Later this year the people of our country will elect the men and women who will govern them at the local, state and national levels.

"While as broadcasters we have direct responsibilities to the candidates for office, let us take a special interest in our even larger concern for the general welfare. If your candidates do not adequately present the issues, let us do so. If the candidates are timid in their advocacy of good, let us say so. If the candidates are squeamish in opposing the wrong, let us have no fear in disclosing it, so all can see and hear and understand.

"An election is the grand climax of democracy. It is the people's central control mechanism. Democracy is brought to the proving ground on every election day. If the people are not there — or if they are not well informed — or not well motivated — our system fails."

The photographic possibilities in politics are endless. Cover political meetings, film legislators visiting the governor, interview the men of power in the party. The sound-on-film camera can be the politician's best friend; or his worst enemy.

The Tie-In

Small towns have trouble getting doctors. That doesn't sound as if it has much possibility for a photo story, but Jack Perkins did a piece on this subject which was aired on the "Huntley-Brinkley Report."

Here's the way he covered it. The one doctor on an island off the coast of Virginia left for another position. The island, in Chesapeake Bay, has a population of less than a thousand. When a person gets sick there the nearest doctor now is 15 miles away by boat.

Perkins and a camera crew visited the island, and this is the story they shot. First, film of the boat leaving for shore (this presented a problem). Next, film showing the small town, its character, the houses and stores. One of the town's three cars was shown as it journeyed down a narrow road, without license plate. The state police never come to Tangiers (there's no crime there) so they don't need state plates.

The clip included a sound-on-film discussion of the problem by two women of the doctorless town. In another sound clip a state health department representative explained the problem: "You must find a doctor whose wife wants to live on a small island."

The dramatic sequence at the end was taken at the church. Sound-on-film of the pastor praying for a doctor. The film ended with the children's choir singing a hymn.

There is, as we all know, a shortage of doctors in small towns. A problem affecting every area of the country. That's the story Jack Perkins reported. He told the story in human terms as it touched one town. You can use this same approach.

The Routine Story is Seldom Routine

Many routine stories develop into dramatic news stories. Here are two examples covered by the authors:

Both Atkins and Willette were on hand when Negro singer Nat "King" Cole sang at the Birmingham Municipal Auditorium. As he sang, several men ran to the stage and attacked him. Willette had his camera ready for anything and got the only pictures of the attack. They were stills, but they were used on CBS. Atkins called in the story for the New York Daily News and it was the lead story in the paper the following morning. The next day Atkins filmed Cole leaving Birmingham, for use by Movietone News.

A story has impact because it is different. The following is the script of a story the authors covered:

"The Goat Man is dead. The Goat Man's body was found in the barbed-wire-surrounded house near Tarrant City, Alabama. Acting Coroner J. L. Boggan said the Goat Man died of natural causes, 'because no one could have gotten to him.' Here Tarrant Police Chief Clyde Sellers looks over the hermit home. The Goat Man got his name years ago when he rode around town in a cart drawn by four goats. For some reason he had nothing to do with other people. He hid in his small house in the woods, locks on the doors, fences surrounding the house. There was a wire fence over the top of the tin roof to catch the stones small boys threw at the house. The Goat Man died as he lived . . . alone. They found the body on the floor. The police had to weave through dark, narrow passageways to find the body."

The tip came from UPI wire which ran a short story that a man known as the Goat Man was found dead. There was a sentence about his fortress house. That was the key to the possibilities of a moving photographic story.

The film included a long shot from a hill above the house, showing the fortress; then photos of the police chief looking around the house. Next, several shots of the fences and the locked door; then inside, for photos of the eerie passageways. The end showed boys looking sad as they stood watching the Goat Man's house.

Change is News

Don't miss the stories of change in your area. Local stations, like the newspapers, too often miss the important stories of change right at home. James Reston, of the New York Times, says: "Like officials in Washington, we suffer from Afghanistanism. If it's far away, it's news, but if it's close at home, it's sociology."

"Something seems to be wrong with the press," Reston said. "I think we are in trouble because we have not kept up with the needs of the age. Change is the biggest story in the world today, and we are not covering it adequately; change in the size and movement of our people; change in the nature, location, and availability of jobs; violent change in the cities and on the land; change in the relations between village and town, town and city, city and state, state and nation, and, of course, change in the relations between empires that are falling and empires that are rising, the old states that are going down and the new ones that are coming up."

Photograph the story of change in your city. This is the most important story you will ever film.

Chapter 5

SHOOTING THE STORY

Perhaps this nation's most tragic, but best-covered story was the assassination of President John F. Kennedy. Both RTNDA and Sigma Delta Chi, professional journalistic fraternities, gave their awards for superior coverage of the tragedy and follow-up angles to WBAP-TV, Fort Worth, Texas.

WBAP-TV News Director Jim Byron tried to analyze what he and his photographers had done to win top honors. He decided that the most important thing his team did was to plan ahead and anticipate. "In almost all cases," said Byron, "our reporters also are cameramen. For the earlier arrival and motorcade story, we had drawn up a rather detailed routine to follow; with specific instructions on what to do should 'something unscheduled happen.' "

Learn to Anticipate

Many of the best pictures and films ever recorded come as the result of talent that is half-instinct, and half-training: the ability to anticipate. Often, this anticipation-factor pays off after the initial story is in the can. Here are a few examples:

City council meeting — a rather routine 100 feet are exposed. Then the cameraman notices tempers heating. He reloads. This is the cameraman who always wants to stay longer, "just in case." He is the one who gets the dramatic film as two warring councilmen nearly come to blows.

Basketball game — after shooting 100 feet of action and cut-aways, the thinking cameraman senses this is going to be a close one. He anticipates that the most colorful scene may come with the final buzzer. It does, and fans pour from the stands, as cheerleaders hug players, as players carry coach.

Co-author Willette won a trophy recently for a still photo taken after a championship prize fight. Purely for his own amusement, Willette shot some

41

25 exposures of 35mm film of the boxing action. At the sound of the final bell, most of the cameramen started putting away their equipment. But Willette anticipated something might develop in the way of a "reaction shot."

It did. After an agonizing few minutes, hometown fighter Ralph Dupas heard the decision — the world championship that had long eluded him was finally his. Willette was able to get only one exposure in the brief instant when the fighter knelt in gratitude, but the photo — "Thanks for My Crown" — was hailed as the sports picture of the year by the New Orleans Press Club.

Be Aggressive

Former RTNDA President Bill Monroe has been news director at the medium-level market (WDSU-TV, New Orleans) and at the larger market, as Director of NBC News, Washington, D. C. As far as spot news is concerned, Monroe offers this advice:

"In shooting the fast-breaking story, the first rule for a cameraman is to be aggressive in getting on top of the action. News producers love the cameraman who has the reputation of getting into the middle of the riot, across the street from the fire, and down the throat of the visiting actress."

The *Reel* Pro

Ask any television newsman what his biggest challenge is, and he will usually reply, "Time." In that day-to-day race against the clock, the minute-hand never rests. It is a relentless enemy. Bruce Palmer, News Director, KWTV, Oklahoma City, gives this example:

"Newscast time is 6 p.m. Then at 5:20 an oiltank truck explodes 47 blocks from the newsroom. We're in luck, as Car number 3 is only half-a-mile from the scene. Our man is on the scene in minutes. He bangs out a terrific 100 feet and streaks for the station. On the way he gives the facts by mobile-radio to a writer; four men killed, six employes and three customers of a nearby business injured. . . .

"Our man hits the lab on the run. At 5:59, one minute before air time, the film is out. It's the lead story of the newscast and the script is ready. We're going to run the thick end of that 100 feet of hot film.

"It goes without saying that every piece of newsfilm ought to be edited on the bench. That's where the best job can be done. But when news is scheduled for 6 o'clock and the viewer habit says, 'News at six,' the shop's best efforts are demanded. The difference can be editing-in-the-camera — complete with cut-aways. It's the mark of a real professional cameraman-reporter."

Always take into consideration the station news schedule. If the schedule is tight and little time exists between coverage and newscast, then editing-in-the-camera *is* the mark of the professional.

Don't always shoot the obvious. Co-author Leo Willette took this prize-winning photo of a fighter before the fight. The other photographers were waiting for the action. This is a main rule of TV news photography: look for the unusual scene. This scene would have made a good beginning for a news clip of the fight.

The TV news photographer must always be ready to shoot. Atkins shot this Confederate flag just as a flaming arrow was fired through it. A dramatic shot was made because the photographer was ready, waiting for something to happen. It was a college prank.

When Birmingham closed its parks, the photographers had to find a way to tell the story. Part of the story were the empty parks. Another part was the workmen actually nailing up the windows of the community centers.

Subjects change. This year photographers are taking film of rockets and other space-age subjects.

While the television news photographer is now trying for complete portability, there still are times when he must steady his long lens on a tripod. Here photographers await a missile firing.

Photo Courtesy of WBZ-TV, Boston

Dick Smilgis, of WBZ-TV news, is shown shooting a fire at Revere, Mass., outside Boston.

The newsfilm photographer may have to photograph anything, even the new snake a· the zoo.

You may shoot a shooting when making newsfilm. Here a woman shoots a cigar from the mouth of a brave smoker. The feature was on a woman's volunteer army.

Sometimes the foreground, such as this tennis net, adds to the picture. You may want to show objects that tell the story, such as the net, when photographing people.

Or you may want to do away with the foreground, in this case, the net-like cage. For this effect, Atkins went inside the lions' cage.

Joe Vadala, NBC cameraman, points out that even the network cameraman must sometimes edit in the camera.

Framing — The most common framing device is the limb or branch of a tree. Notice in the drawing of the boat how the monotony of the water and sky is broken by framing them with the tree.

The rule-of-thirds applies to vertical objects, too. In this drawing of a lighthouse, note how its vertical lines fill in the left one-third of the picture.

Oversweep — TV cuts as much as one-eighth from your film, so you have to play it safe and leave extra space when shooting. On the left, the face as you shot it; on the right, the way it may come out on TV. The shaded area would not show.

Rule-of-Thirds — This uncomplicated compositional element simply means that not every subject has to be centered. Horizons need not cut the frame of your picture in half. Horizons should occupy either the top or bottom third of the picture. In the drawing of the jet aircraft, notice how the horizontal lines of the plane occupy the lower third of the picture.

Framing can set the scene for the viewer. Here the story is on highway construction. An old wheel and fence are used as a frame. Construction in the background.

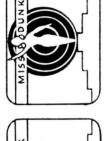

Into Frame — To give sequence to a film of five girls in a beauty contest, use "into frame" technique, which records the subject as it enters the frame. You would not want to pan the contestants as they marched by.

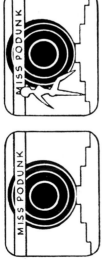

Out of Frame — This is the same technique, except the subject is leaving the scene. As in the drawings below, the man walks out of the picture as the camera stays fixed. If this man is going to walk 100 feet, shoot him walking out of frame, then show him at his destination in the next sequence.

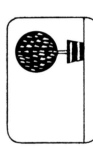
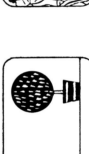

False Reverse — If you shoot film of people coming and going, you will get a false reverse. The girl below would march one way, then the next cut would show her marching the other way. This could also happen when cutting film shot from opposite sides of the street.

Exception to the rule — Although this picture violates almost every rule of newsfilm photography, it is compositionally and artistically attractive, and most important, tells the story. Larry Lala, of WWL-TV, captured the loneliness and the stark drama of death after a barge knocked out a section of this causeway sending seven bus passengers to their deaths. Here is a long shot that is backlighted and lacks the obvious human element. Yet Lala's picture observed most artistic rules, especially the rule-of-thirds.

Photo courtesy of NBC

NBC newsmen are shown on location in Iran. The networks now send photographers and crews all over the world to film news stories and documentaries.

Always look for the different angle. Here Ken Williams, of Chrysler, plans for photographers to make aerial photos from a helicopter.

Though cameras are becoming more portable, cameramen still use a tripod for heavy sound cameras.

Sometimes the cameraman must use a car as a dolly. Here NBC news photographers shoot the main street of a small town.

F I L L   O U T

FREELANCERS WILL NEED THE FOLLOWING INFORMATION:

The type(s) of film(s) we use (is-are):

DAYLIGHT   **TUNGSTEN AND POOR LIGHT**

Type_____   Type_____
ASA Rating_____   ASA Rating_____
Other Rating_____   Other Rating_____
Filter Preference_____   Other Directions_____
Filter Factor_____f stops   _____
Other Directions _____   _____
_____   _____
_____   _____

The Monday thru _____Times, Titles and Processing-Editing

Deadlines of our news shows are

TIME: TITLE: DEADLINE: SPECIAL STORY NEEDS:

_____   _____   _____   _____
_____   _____   _____   _____
_____   _____   _____   _____
_____   _____   _____   _____

Weekend or other Scheduled Special News Programming:

Day & Time:_____ ; Title: _____; Deadline: _____

Special Needs: _____.

STAFF PHONE NUMBERS   TITLE: OFFICE PHONE: HOME PHONE:
    NAME:

_____   _____   _____   _____
_____   _____   _____   _____
_____   _____   _____   _____

Film Shipment Instructions to Stringers:

_____
_____

Mind in Motion

When it comes to newsfilm, few in the business touch as many bases as does Howard Back. Back has a background that includes the academic (master's degree in journalism from Ohio State) ; basic news (both with newspaper and radio) ; newsfilm (news editor for Telenews-Hearst Metrotone News) ; producer of film products (manager, motion pictures, radio, and television, Chrysler Corporation) ; and public relations-newsfilm (executive editor of National Television News in Detroit).

Back says that the cameraman and editor must work toward the final, polished product. "The newsfilm cameraman must know the rules of logical continuity. Each story he shoots must have a beginning, a middle, and an end. He must shoot scenes so that they can be edited in a logical progression and permit the viewer to see what the viewer expects to see. He must provide a variety of camera angles, he must establish his location, he must provide logical transition shots.

"Somebody," says Back, "once quoted the old Chinese philosopher about a picture being worth a thousand words. If that's true, then a minute of (well-edited) newsfilm, with 1,440 frames or pictures, should be worth 1,440,000 words.

"So think. To paraphrase the old Chinese philosopher again: Before you open your lens, be sure your mind is in motion."

Panning

If there is any one quality to a film story which brands it as the work of a non-professional, that quality is over-panning. It is to the neophyte and bush-league cameraman what "tromboning" is to the men with the new zoom lenses.

Over-panning and over-zooming are annoying, distracting, unnecessary, amateurish, shaky, uneven, and disconcerting. They result in film that is difficult, if not impossible, to edit.

Over-panning has probably cost more jobs than alcohol, and some news directors and film editors have had to issue orders: "Don't pan!" We don't know why . . . but all newcomers to newsfilm want to pan. And pan. And pan. They never seem to pan out.

Certainly, there is a place for the pan in news photography. How else can one follow action? A pan helps in showing the size and scope of scene, but when you pan, do it slowly and smoothly.

Space Age

A decade ago an assignment to cover a shot to the moon would have been just short of fantasy. Yet, today, hundreds of TV cameramen can boast of being veterans of "Birdwatch Beach" — having filmed more launches at Cape Kennedy than they can shake a tripod at.

Since many more hundreds of cameramen will be joining the birdwatching ranks in the decade to come, Ron Oppen (cameraman, WTVJ, Miami) offers these missile-shooting tips:

"Normally, I use anything from a six to a 10-inch lens, depending upon the size of the missile and distance from the pad. The normal distance is about one-and-a-quarter miles. I use a hydraulic tripod head on a pro-junior. The head costs about $225.00 and is excellent for all kinds of shooting.

"At the same time I shoot the launching with the long lens on a motor-driven Bell & Howell 70 DH. I also shoot sound film at the same time with an Auricon 100-footer. I have both cameras sighted. The Auricon starts at T-minus 15 seconds. The silent camera starts at T-minus 10 seconds.

"The sound camera is in a fixed position. It takes a wide shot of the missile rising up in a cloud of smoke, climbing out of frame. I also get the natural SOF of the countdown and the tremendous roar, which adds immensely to the audio-visual value of the story."

Accident Coverage

Most educators do not necessarily turn their academic noses skyward at the thought of accident coverage. Most instructors and journalists know this is a legitimate and common element to most news programs. Accident coverage brings with it to the screen the safety lesson that carries the nagging hope most newsmen harbor: that someone watching might prevent tomorrow's accident. Educators, however, do feel that routine accident coverage looks exactly like that — routine. Routine and predictable and usually showing nothing more than a mass of tangled metal.

At the University of Missouri's School of Journalism, Assistant Professor Rod Gelatt offers this suggestion:

"If it involves a youngster on a tricycle hit by a car — why not a low-angle shot of the tricycle, then a tilt-up to frame the car in the background, through the handle-bars?"

Fire Coverage

Deservedly or not, Boston "enjoys" the reputation of having more fires than any other city. Who is better qualified, then, to discuss shooting fires than Boston News Director Ed Fouhy, of WBZ-TV?

"My pet peeve on fire films," he says, "is that the cameramen are always so fascinated by the flames, they don't shoot the people. Recently a two-alarmer did considerable damage to a local college dormitory. As usual, our stringer came back with plenty of smoke and flames, but missed the story. The real story was that the students forced out included a singing group. This singing group promptly began to serenade the fire fighters. Our film had no pics of the students or the singers."

Fouhy echoes the recurring theme, scattered throughout this book: "Shoot the people." The rookie cameraman on the beat should certainly get shots of firemen and fire chiefs in action. This makes friends, as well as good newsfilm. There is a little ham in all of us — and the fire captain who is made to look hard-working and dramatic on TV will think several times before ordering cameramen far behind fire lines.

To quote Fouhy: "For drama there's nothing like a shot of three firemen braced against a bucking hose. And the cameraman who shoots tight, tight close-ups of firemen's faces as they take off their smoke masks after hard work inside a burning building always gets my vote."

Color

One does not have to be a visionary to predict that soon, most news, feature, and documentary film shot for television in this country will be shot in color.

Color has been used regularly for feature films for over four years by Co-author Willette on his top-ranked Sunday night news program. At other times, WWL-TV and WDSU-TV (both New Orleans) have gone all out and have geared color film into their daily news budget, primarily because of nearby color labs at Pan-American Films. But unfortunately this has usually been for promotional purposes.

While many stations would have trouble getting spot news color films developed, stations can now shoot features and documentaries in color. Processing black and white film is now a commonplace affair in most news departments. Color processing, though, introduces equipment, chemicals, narrow tolerances, know-how, and financial expenditures that will keep it out of newsrooms for some years to come.

Color newsfilm can be farmed out to commercial labs, when they are available. Curiously enough, the speed of color film is no longer much of a deterrent from adapting color to newsfilm coverage. The color newscast is as inevitable as tomorrow's dawn. And just as much bursting with bright realism, too.

Shoot the Follow-Up

One of the more knowledgeable newsmen to speak out against one failure of TV news is Joseph Loughlin, Director of News, WCBS-TV, New York City.

"I don't believe local television — and I'm talking about local television everywhere I have worked — does a good job on the follow-up," says Loughlin. "The ball is dropped not only on routine follow-up stories, but I've seen frequent cases of stations failing to follow up stories they have broken themselves.

"I know of one case where a station broke a major economic story, probably the most important economic break of the year for that particular market, but failed to follow it up or give it to the wire services. A morning daily 'broke' the same story a month later with a banner headline."

Loughlin believes there are three basic reasons why TV news mishandles the follow-up, as follows: "Pressure: In our hurry to broadcast on the air every day, we too often forget about what happened yesterday and what might be in the cards tomorrow.

"Lack of Confidence: Too many television news people still feel that they are not in the same league with newspapermen. They are afraid to break new ground (and break new stories) without first checking the wires of the news-paper. Ridiculous, but true. In other words, they think some anonymous guy across town has better editorial judgment, even when it comes to their own product. Unbelievable!

"Staffing: Television still does not have enough special reporters, particularly of the investigative type. Moreover, few newsrooms that I've seen have anything approaching a research set-up and morgue."

Think Overall

Someone once made a lot of money by selling a sign that says: "Think Big." The person who wrote that sign was thinking of big profits. And, of course, it is always much easier to offer advice than to take it.

But, the authors offer a summing up of advice: (1) learn the mechanics of shooting, (2) learn to think of the entire story when shooting.

Bob Spearman, instructor, School of Journalism, University of Nebraska (Lincoln, Neb.) says he tells his students: "Shoot the film, look at the film, write the story, edit the film, read the story while looking at the film."

You'll learn to shoot good film by following this advice.

Chapter 6

SOUND

Simply using sound is not always an improvement on silent coverage; but when someone has something to say, or there are natural sounds to be captured which help communicate the story, then use the sound camera or the tape recorder.

Magnetic sound is quickly replacing optical sound. Most sound cameras can be converted to record magnetic sound. Optical sound is a jagged picture of sound. A flickering light records the sound on the edge of the film. Magnetic sound is recorded just as in a tape recorder. A thin strip of tape is added to the film edge. Magnetic sound, unlike optical sound, is not affected by processing. The quality is vastly better than optical sound.

For optical sound, it is best to experiment to find which sound index number produces the best quality. For example, for Du Pont 931A Reversal, the sound index would likely be $11\frac{1}{2}$. For negative film of the same exposure speed, the sound index would be $10\frac{1}{2}$. The slower the speed, the higher the sound index.

For magnetic sound use the manufacturer's recommendation for level control. The sound is regulated on the VU meter.

Hal Saylor, photographer, WTOP-TV, Washington, D. C., says that magnetic sound results in better quality. He also points out that it is much easier to edit.

"By using a magnetic pencil you can erase sound," Saylor says, "and you can add sound to magnetic sound."

Sound Advice

Can sound-on-film be used incorrectly?

Of course. And Professor Dick Yoakam, Indiana University, feels that SOF is getting more and more "perverted," as more and more stations get more and more SOF equipment. Yoakam is an educator, RTNDA member and officer, and a frequent judge in newsfilm contests. Furthermore, Yoakam is the former news director at KCRG-TV, in Cedar Rapids, Iowa. No words-mincer, Yoakam's charge of SOF "perversion" is explained this way:

"In the old days, when we had to illustrate a difficult story, we had to shoot narrative-documentary form — and try to make the narration and the picture tell the story. . . . For example, the new fire truck came to town and we had the chief run the ladder up, and we took shots of the hands on the dials, and the man climbing the ladder . . . and we followed the production unities of the motion picture newsfilm very carefully.

"Now, today, the new wagon comes to town and the local TV reporter goes out with his portable Auricon, stands the chief in front of the wagon and asks him, 'What about this new wagon?' The chief then answers how much it cost in so many dollars, that it can reach to a ninth floor window, and that it's going to be a great boon to his department.

"Nowhere in this shot is a picture of the machine at work with all of its fascinating possibilities . . . for the visual."

Yoakam makes a stunning point here. "I recently viewed a story of the dedication of a $10,000,000 library. The entire sequence was made up of a series of men in academic gowns making speeches about the library.

"There was not a single shot of the interior of the library, not of a book, nor of any of the wonderful modern devices. . . . Here the sound on film was used in a most perverted way — to obscure the story and simply to show a bunch of big-wigs making fatuous remarks."

Simple Double System

"Sound film of a subject in front of the camera talking can get pretty dull visually," says Stan Vainrib, WBBM, Chicago. "If a reporter or news subject is talking about a fire which destroyed a furniture store there should be photographs of the fire and the aftermath rather than a picture of the man talking at the scene." There are two easy and effective ways to do this:

(1) Use a small portable tape recorder. Shoot your film; edit a short (say, five-second) strip of the person interviewed or reporter to the head of the film; use this silent film, say of the ruins of a fire, and run the tape under. This gives you good sound that is easy to edit.

(2) Another system is to have the reporter (or person interviewed) make his sound statement. Take notes as he talks. When he says, "the building," "all the windows were smashed," or "$100,000 worth of chairs were destroyed," make a note of it. Then shoot these shots on silent film. You run the sound film on one projector and the silent on another. You can time the film so that you cut from the sound film to the silent and run it through, or you can cue various scenes and punch them in at the proper time. Time the shots so the photo of the building will be shown when he says "building," the film of the window when he says "window."

Most sound cameras now manufactured can be modified to record magnetic sound. Here, the Auricon is so adapted. The unit is portable.

Here are some examples using the same story, the furniture store fire:

The sound film of the reporter describing what happened will be running. As he says, "The building" the other roll (silent film) is started and the silent film put on the air. The sound is used as narration. If the film is edited to fit the entire film, the silent will run through.

Or it can be done this way. As the reporter says, "the building," switch to the silent shot of the building; then after several seconds go back to the picture of the reporter talking. As the reporter continues he will hit another key phrase, such as, "the windows were smashed." At this point the silent film is again used. You have double-system sound with cut-aways, with no time-consuming expensive lab work.

Two Sounds Sound Better

There are times when two different sound-on-film ingredients can be woven together with startling results.

When Dick John was directing TV news in Oklahoma City, one of the big stories he faced was one for which he could prepare and plan ahead — the end of statewide prohibition. With the end of this dry-spell, naturally, would come the start of a wet-spell: the first day of legal liquor.

Outside one of the largest liquor outlets in Oklahoma City, John had a sound-on-film camera recording a group of "dry" ladies singing "Onward Christian Soldiers." Inside the store cash registers were ringing merrily. And John's SOF cameras recorded the *bringg* of the register while the picture portion of the film offered ECU shots of the sales amounts: $4.56 . . . $12.87 . . . $8.50, and various figures in the picture, but the soundtrack portion stayed the same — a double *bringg-bringg*.

Later in the editing room, someone hit upon the idea of combining the two main ingredients into something of a fugue, with cash registers in counterpoint with the ladies' voices!

"Onward Christian Soldiers . . ."
Bringg-bringgg . . .
"Marching as to War . . ."
Bringg-Bringgg . . .

The result not only told the story, but had almost a Morality Play simplicity: Good Dry Ladies versus Bad Demon Rum (who was dancing merrily to the accompaniment of music composed for the Almighty Dollar).

This was a sound-on-film classic.

Need a Reporter?

Joe Epley, of WBT-TV, Charlotte, N. C., says of sound:

"One item which I think makes for better newsfilm is keeping the reporter out of the picture unless necessary. News conferences and give-and-take interviews need the reporter. But if the individuals concerned can tell what happened, or you can pick up the natural SOF of their conversations without putting a reporter between the camera and the subject, your film report becomes much more effective."

The Dramatic Sound

In the use of sounds and their relationships with narration, it is well to remember that sounds and words can work together; complementing each other.

CBS Reporter Dan Rather once did a splendid and gripping sound on film report on the opening of a "bomb-proof" underground school; certainly symptomatic of fearsome times. In the report Rather included a short interview with a local official giving the reason for this underground grade school and a moving interview with a very young little girl who explained in childish innocence how she faced the first grade in a steel-encased, windowless schoolroom. But the most bizarre, 1984ish quality of the story came when Rather and his cameraman combined to clang shut the massive steel doors of this "tomb." The hollow, subterranean and sepulchral sounds and reverberations sent shivers up the spine.

For the final few seconds, Reporter Rather didn't say a word. He didn't have to. The sounds had told the story much more eloquently.

Wild Sound

Educator John Rider would like to see greater use of "wild sound." Rider is an assistant professor in the Television and Radio Center of Syracuse University.

As far as natural background sounds, he suggests: "Let's get some 'wild sound' to give background. In fact, we can hedge on SOF if we get wild sound to support the newscaster talking about what the speaker said, or describing the event."

Using Tape

Not all sound, or even the best sound, is necessarily sound on film. As portable tape recorders get more miniaturized and as they produce better and better fidelity, their use in the newsroom gets more varied and more in demand.

The key words on portable tape might seem to be: "natural sounds" . . . background effects . . . a mood-creating device which really adds another dimension toward the viewer (and listener) being there.

Imagine shooting a parade with the customary sound on film rig? You would either face the job of anchoring-down the sound camera and the resultant monotony of film shot from one basic angle, or you would have the nerve shattering job of piecing together a dozen elements of film — each of which would have its own complementing sound ingredient.

The sound camera is now found at public meetings in every large city. It goes just about everywhere the newspaper reporter goes.

In other words, in editing for picture, the man at the editing table might use a dozen scenes, angles, cutaways, cut-ins, and other devices; but when the sound track hit the air it would be a hodge-podge of different bands, two seconds of marching feet, three seconds of a tank rumbling by, some disconnected (and disconcerting) cheers, and a seven-second sputter of a police officer's motorcycle. Even if the picture made sense the sound would not.

In New Orleans, portable tapes have been the answer to covering events like funeral parades — where the colorful musicians meander all over a neighborhood after having returned from the cemetery and made farewells to a fallen friend. But parades are only one example of how natural background sounds, music, or effects can be added to film.

Most cameramen simply strap the recorders to their belts, pin the small microphone to a jacket lapel, press the "record" button, and then let it roll. Usually on the way back to the newsroom, the cameraman can play back the tape and start judging the merits of different "takes." (A playback is a must. You can never tell when some expletive or obscenity might have floated into your equipment.)

By all means, check with the station audio engineer *before* buying any audio equipment. This man usually knows of all the latest equipment and improvements. Then, too, chances are he can get you a good price. Remember, your audio men are going to have to work with this tape, too. So set up certain standards as to speed and volume level. Don't ever be afraid of "annoying" an audio man by talking audio. Most of them devour any opportunity to talk sound (just as any good lensman does in talking cameras and film).

One other thing: the difference between "sound" and "noise." Sound is anything you want. Noise is anything you don't want.

Chapter 7

THE FEATURE

"Features," defined one Midwestern TV news director, "are what people jump up to watch . . . are moved by . . . talk about . . . respond to . . . and remember. I hate 'em."

And why should this news director hate features? Candidly, he explained: "My competition does a damn better job on them than we do."

Now the key words to the appeal of the feature film story are found in his first statement: people watch, react to, and recall features; they are motivated and touched by them.

Furthermore, if certain features are frame-worked well and run regularly — same day, same time — people will tune to the news program which offers this TV treat. And remember this about straight news: not a single person in the vast TV audience has ever turned to his wife in the evening and said: "Let's tune into the evening news and see their coverage of today's luncheons and the city council meeting." It is doubtful that anyone ever will.

Yet TV features are often maligned, sloughed off, discouraged, or merely tolerated. As one very excellent newsman once said to us: "Features are those stories which a newscast can darn well do without." In other words, features to him were fillers; to be used only when hard news had failed to fill his 15 minutes.

Why this distaste? Only one reason is apparent: many news editors, news directors, and news cameramen simply lack the talent, imagination, creativity, or energy to produce them. The very cameraman least capable of producing a creditable feature is the same one in every news department who knocks someone else's product by loudly and smugly proclaiming: "That's not news." (Then this same cameraman edits *his* contribution to that day's news program: two luncheon meetings and a fender-scraping.)

Let us examine the oft-heard suggestion that features are not news. One

Southwestern news director who boasts a powerful rating and an enormous influence on his community got into this discussion one time at a national RTNDA convention.

"In my town," he said, "news is what I say is news. And I don't depend on the news judgment of some afternoon newspaper's editor to do my selecting.

"Sure, we'll both cover a lot of the same stories — fires, fatal accidents, big city council sessions, that sort of thing, but if I want to say that today's news includes this film story we put on the air involving a kid having trouble flying a kite, then, in my town, that kid and his kite are news. And if the opposition news director hollers and yells that 'that isn't news,' I respectfully invite him to look over the ratings."

This is not to suggest that our newsman friend ignores hard news. But he uses the feature the way a skillful chef might employ a dessert in rounding out a perfect dinner. No one wants a meal that would be one dessert course after another. But eight courses of meat and potatoes is hardly the answer, either. Hard, important news certainly takes priority in a responsible newscast, but it is the feature which often turns the responsible program into the memorable news program.

At the rate that cameras and films are reducing the human error in filming, the time may well come when a trained chimp can aim a camera and shoot a usable piece of footage on a big fire. Let's face it, a film story of this sort tells itself and rarely requires more than a modicum of imagination. But a well planned, well executed feature film can be a great source of pride and development to the individual cameraman.

In many contests, certain cameramen tend to value especially the prizes they win in the categories of human interest and creativity. Some even prefer these awards to those in the Best Spot News category. Why? Because in spot news it is usually the *story* that wins, not the film. If the story is big enough, important enough, spectacular enough, the winning cameraman will be the one who happened to get there first. His colleagues may thus have been beaten out because of a traffic jam or an untimely day off. In features, on the other hand, it is almost always the *film* which wins; and the story structure is merely the vehicle which frames the cameraman's eye, mind, and heart.

Film Tells the Story

The feature comes closest to perfection when the film defies the spoken voice — when the picture says to the writer, "Who needs you?"

One of the most talked about stories ever shot by a certain television station offered only this much narration before the film (with music under) rolled its way into the minds and hearts of the viewers:

"This is a story which needs no words other than these: It's the tale of a little boy on a long, long summer's day."

With this the film showed a "typical" American youngster bursting out

70

the front door of his home. . . . A reverse shot follows his turning head as he glances around for other kids . . . the streets are empty . . . the boy turns to his dog . . . the dog turns away. It's too hot . . . the boy takes off down the sidewalk. . . . He spots a rock. . . . Boy being boy, he kicks the rock down the sidewalk (with a couple of extreme closeups (ECU's) of sneaker meeting rock). . . . Tired of this, the boy reaches down and puts rock in already bulging pocket. . . . Into frame, out of frame across a field. . . . Use of low angle allows boy to rise into view atop crest of hill. . . . Over the shoulder shows boy looking over river. . . . River boats go by. . . . Old man rows by as boy waves. . . . Oldtimer waves back. . . . Reverse ECU shows beaming boy. . . .

Low angle shows large, driftwood log . . . boys runs into frame   balances as he trots across log . . . runs out of frame. . . . Into scene of fence runs boy, climbing fence, looking . . . over the shoulder shows cows grazing. . . . Closeup (CU) boy, then out of frame . . . boy runs down small rise, alongside stream . . . in bushes, finds stick fishing-pole. . . . Medium Closeup (MCU) boy casting. . . . ECU line and cork hits water. . . . Long Shot (LS) boy fidgety waiting for bite. . . . ECU non-bobbing cork. . . . LS boy hurls pole into stream. . . . CU pole sinks. . . . Medium Long Shot (MLS) boy running into frame across field. . . . Medium Shot (MS) twisted tree and trunk. . . . MS reverse as boy scales tree, resting in crook of treelimbs. . . . CU boy's hand reaches into shirt, extracting space comic book. . . . ECU cover of comic book. . . . ECU wide-eyed, thoroughly absorbed boy. . . . Extra Long Shot (XLS) conclusion shot, boy resting and reading. (Music: up to conclusion.)

Hurrah for Holidays

Just about all of us like holidays. You might say, this is "The American Way," and this affection for holidays carries over into most newsrooms. The only trouble is that after a few years of holiday film-stories, not only the audience, but writer and cameraman all seem to be saying: "Excuse me please, this is where I came in."

The truth is that although most of us like these holidays, they roll around with annoying frequency. The techniques and ideas we first used years ago have become habit-forming. We have created another "Celluloid Cliche."

You have seen these. Note how predictable the season becomes:

Christmas Shopping — "clever" fast-motion photography of shoppers. Last Day of School — "clever" fast-motion photography, perhaps with musical accompaniment of "William Tell Overture" as an added fillip. Thanksgiving Day — the hackneyed scene of a "typical" American family gathered around the roasted turkey, with a freckle-faced boy holding knife and fork straight up at 90 degrees from table. This is not only rather trite, but usually comes off with a "hokey" look about it — no one believes it was not shot two days before (which it was). New Year's Day — the city's first born in the "Diaper Derby" or "Stork Parade" or whatever it is called locally. And don't forget that "morning after" tableau — cigarette butts, empty glasses, confetti, and discarded silly hats. (Come now. Does *everybody* wear silly hats at New Year's Eve parties?)

Why not try something different and experimental? Why not storyboard an entire holiday story of unusual angles and different approaches; then go out and find the scenes to fit your storyboard. And why not treat one of these holidays with a bit of whimsey? They don't all have to be solemn.

For example, one Thanksgiving (at WWL-TV, New Orleans) co-author Willette (helped by some sound on film cut-ins) "interviewed" a turkey on the day before Thanksgiving. After each question by the newsman the film editor spliced in some SOF gobbles. Then, after each gobble, Willette would repeat what the turkey had "commented." "Oh, you say you just haven't got that old holiday spirit. Tell me, whatever became of your cousin, the fellow I interviewed here last year?" (Gobble, gobble!) "Oh really, I'm very sorry to hear that. Well I suppose you are planning a big Christmas." (Gobble, gobble!) "You say you've made no plans for Christmas? Do you mean you plan to be out of town?" (Gobble, gobble!) "Oh I see, you are planning for a holiday that will be 'out of this world.' " And so on.

In this case, cameraman Mike O'Connor "pre-interviewed" the turkey. That is, he thrust his camera and microphone into the bird's wooden pen. Just the appearance of this apparatus in his cage was enough to inspire about 30 feet of good gobbles from the "interviewee." These SOF close-ups of the turkey were then cut into short and expressive "takes" and spliced in following each question by Willette.

Though falling short of masterpiece level, it was fun, it broke the boredom barrier, and it provided Willette with a certain identity. ("Oh, you're the guy who talks to turkeys!")

Great Day for Groundhogging

Along the same lines, the same newsman once went through an entire interview with a zoo director who was explaining all about Groundhog Day — noting the shadow on the ground and all that. The interview was done entirely straight-faced, *a la* Bob and Ray. Only trouble was that throughout the interview the subject was obviously a kangaroo, not a groundhog.

Toward the end, the reporter nervously spoke: "Well, that's fine. So the shadow means more winter. Thank you. But . . . ah . . . there's one little thing I'd like to clear up in my mind. I . . . ah . . . don't wish to seem like a wise-guy or anything . . . but . . . our subject looks suspiciously like a kangaroo."

The zoo director had been prepped and replied: "Why of course it does. It *is* a kangaroo."

"But isn't that sort of like . . . fudging a little . . . using a kangaroo instead of a groundhog?" asked the newsman.

"Well," explained the zoo director, "the groundhog we had died a few weeks ago . . . and I was hoping you wouldn't notice. Besides . . . the working principle's the same anyway. Maybe the shadow's a little bigger. . . ."

Sometimes just a different kind of opening and closing will transport the routine holiday story from blah to zowie!

One Fourth of July in New Orleans, Newsman Willette and Cameraman Del Hall teamed for this flavorful holiday morsel — using a sound-on-film opening and closing with the middle portion narrative supplied on tape by Willette at the station while "on the air."

VIDEO	AUDIO
Live News Announcer:	It's hardly the news scoop of the year that today was a big day to millions of Americans. In fact, the biggest to those who wish to honor America's birthday — The Fourth of July.
	For a round-up on the "Fourth" in New Orleans... this report by newsman Leo Willette.
Sound on Film: *Shows newsman seated in beach chair, languidly sipping a huge and colorful drink, while two bikini-clad beauties fan him — a third ready to attend to his every wish such as holding drink*	This is Leo Willette, reporting on this Fourth of July story from where the going is the thickest. Because dedicated newsmen, you see, must work on holidays.
	We try not to complain too much. It's just part of the harrowing life we must staunchly brave.
Audio Tape Over Silent Film	
Various shots, cars on the go	For luckier Americans, however, today was a day of rest, relaxation, and fun.
	It was a day of everyone on the go.
	Over most of the nation, city people were heading to the country....
	Country people were heading for the city.... Mountain residents rushed to the seashore and those who live near the beaches headed for the hills.

Then, by word and picture, this feature carried the viewer to a yacht basin, a golf course, a patriotic ceremony, the barbecuing area of a city park, a row boating pond; to a man napping, a "No swimming" section of a beach that had become polluted and made big news a few days earlier (note the followup aspect); to a coed studying, a running shot of a police car, a sleeping baby (you can't go wrong with at least one sleeping baby per holiday); to a "muscle beach" stretch of sand, some pretty girls sun-bathing (you can't go wrong with at least one pretty girl per holiday, either), then back to the scene-setting reporter for the concluding SOF segment.

VIDEO	AUDIO
	All in all . . . a great day. Unless, that is, you had to work.
Sound on Film Portion: *Same scene, reporter with drink and three skimpily attired bathing beauties*	"So . . . while the rest of the nation relaxes, that hardworking, dedicated breed known as newsmen put in another hard day of work." "Pity for a moment . . . if you will . . . The Poor Newsman — pausing in his frantic pursuit of truth to clutch any fleeting moment of relaxation, as best he can."
One beauty leans in pressing drink and straws for newsman's sipping	
After long sip and sigh	"Sleep well America — your newsman is awake!"

Story of a Film Story

"Beauty is in the eye of the beholder." And so is a good feature story. How much chance would you give for a story on a shantytown to win awards and recognition?

One such film story did — a film story shot by Mike O'Connor, while Leo Willette accompanied him for the better part of two days getting the flavor and feel of this area of tar-paper shacks and its "denizens of the driftwood."

In two days of filming and interviewing, O'Connor and Willette came back with more than just a feature; they returned with a feeling, an empathy, even a genuine affection for these people of the shantytown. Every city has its own type of shantytown. In New Orleans, it is called the "Battures."

Note how writer and cameraman teamed their talents to present "The Batture Dwellers."

VIDEO	AUDIO
Announcer over slide:	Tonight a visit to a rather strange colony — a New Orleans type of shantytown; a shantytown made unique and made possible by the river. "The Batture Dwellers."
FILM LS, *Flowing river*	This is the river. The "Father of Waters," as it was called by the Indians. And the "Father of Waters" as it remains today.
LS, *Reverse shot, showing shacks and suggestions of people, smoke from chimneys, small boats, etc.*	For many, many thousands of people and creatures, the river is the giver of life.

CU, *Swirling water around driftwood*

But ... at best ... the river is a kind of treacherous friend: ready to take back in an instant what it has taken centuries to bestow.

LS, *Pan from levee, showing batture dweller shacks*

Perhaps no breed of people know, respect, and hold in awe this river, as do "Batture Dwellers."

MS, *Two shacks, with river in background*

To find a colony of the Batture Dwellers by water, it is necessary only to cruise either the east bank or the west bank of the river around New Orleans.

LS, *Pan from river, showing deep underbrush flowing by to reveal start of shack colony*

It is here . . . where civilization ends . . . that the Batture colony will begin.

The Batture Dwellers we see tonight live just above Walnut Street. Their colony extends from the end of

Shoot the story of people. Willette and cameraman Mike O'Connor shot a two-part series on "The Batture Dwellers," the people who live in New Orleans' Shantytown.

CU, *Water lapping at river's end, muddy and ominous*	the salvage yard around Walnut Street and stretches all along the Batture to the office of the U. S. Engineers at the foot of Prytania. On one side is always the river: sometimes friendly, sometimes angry . . . but always the river. And always there. . . .
MLS, *The levee, from angle which shows its rise from city side, suggesting the tops of shacks and showing how levee keeps river at bay*	On the other side is the levee . . . the end of the city for most of us. But, for the Batture Dwellers it is the "high grounds" which keep out one world, while offering a certain sanctuary inside another world.
MS, *Couple gathering driftwood*	Truly, this is a city within a city.
Various action follows couple as they carry driftwood into colony, laying it alongside their shack	For newcomers here, let's describe now what a "batture" is: A batture is land built-up by the river. For, over the years, the river deposits earth, rocks, driftwood, and debris. A batture, then, is a gift of the river — sometimes welcomed, sometimes unwelcomed.
MS, *Land build-up alongside river* *CU's and ECU's of limbs, rocks, etc.*	This gift includes silt and soil from Minnesota . . . perhaps a twig from St. Joe, Missouri . . . a rusting piece of can from Natchez . . . small stones from the riverbanks of Iowa . . . plus other offerings from Illinois, Tennessee, and Wisconsin. In a poetic sense, a batture is a little piece of half of America.
LS, *Elderly woman pulling cardboard, crossing levee*	The people who take over these battures pay no rent, pay no taxes . . . have very little . . . need very little . . . expect very little.
MS, *Elderly woman pauses to talk with man lounging atop levee*	Their houses can be described a thousand ways, such as "ramshackles" . . . "disgraceful shanties" . . . "an eyesore and blot" . . . "shacks."
CU *of wood sides of various batture dwellings*	And always there is wood. Generally driftwood. The offerings of the "Father of Waters." As we said . . . the Batture dwellings can be called many things.
MLS, *Elderly woman continues her slow walk with cardboard to her shack*	But let us hear how our original note from researcher Gordon Kirst described the Battures:
MS to CU, *Various shots and angles of shacks, especially supporting "legs"*	"They are a row of gaunt and greying structures, standing on tall black pilings — many, precariously, just beyond the river's reach. Grotesque and gawky, they creep along the water's edge, perched on their

76

| | skinny, wooden legs like weak old men on stilts — trying to keep their fragile feet from getting wet." |

VIDEO	AUDIO
MS, *Woman hoeing garden, framed by grotesque trees and hanging Spanish moss*	Some people will tell you tales of these humble dwellings being nothing more than a camouflage on the outside, for mysterious splendors and riches on the inside.
MS and MCU, *Elderly quartet sitting on steps, in background kids playing on river's edge*	This *could* be so (with the possibility of deep freezers, TV, stereo, and art objects inside), but somehow we don't think so. In truth, the *Shades of New Orleans* camera of Mike O'Connor was not invited inside any of the houses, so we can't say for certain.
MS and LS, *various houses*	But talk about eccentrics hiding their wealth in the Batture dwellings appears to be only an interesting and recurring legend, nothing more.
LS and MS, *the river, with driftwood flowing by*	This much tells just half the story of the Battures — the people and the dwellings. Next week, part two of this story of Man and the River; A river that is part-time servant . . . and full-time master.

(Music: up to fill)

On the following week our film story tended to concentrate less on the dwellings and more on the dwellers. The batture, it developed, even had its own church.

Since one episode concentrated heavily on the dwellings, perhaps it would be worthwhile to examine the follow-up story which concentrated more on people.

Since the television newsman can never be certain his viewers saw the previous chapter to a follow-up story, a certain amount of verbal and film "establishing" must be repeated. In other words, each story must stand on its own. Here is the script for Battures, Part Two.

VIDEO	AUDIO
LS, *Establishing shot of river and battures*	Where the river ends . . . often begins a strange kind of colony. This is the colony of an unusual, a rather independent breed of people known as "Batture Dwellers."
MS and CU, *Water lapping ashore* MS, *Woman in small field, bending over from time to time, weeding, then walking on*	From the river these people get almost all things — certainly the river brings them the soil and the moisture for their tiny patches of cultivated land. Here, they grow their greens, their corn, their cabbages, and their collards.

77

CU, *Pigs and chickens eating grain from ground*
MS, *Chicken walking up levee*

Some Batture Dwellers raise animals, too: pigs and chickens mostly. Being river dwellers themselves, these animals scoot for the high ground when the river rises too high.

LS, *Shacks*

Life in the Battures can be described several ways — depending for the most part on one's own attitude.

LS, *Lone man walking down levee, slowly, moodily, alone*

Here, the people are "easy going" ... or they are somewhat "lazy" ... maybe even "shiftless," depending on how one looks at that sort of thing. But certainly life on the Battures is less than frantic.

MS and MCU's, *Two men talking and smoking*

A good conversation here can take the better part of a day (but maybe that's what days were made for anyway).

MLS, *Pan of dwellings, showing patch-work construction, various* MCU's *and* CU's *of woman pulling sheet of cardboard, her mongrel dogs greet her*

One thing is certain: among the Batture Dwellers there is little waste. As the *Shades of New Orleans* camera of Mike O'Connor was recording these scenes, an elderly woman carted home her new-found treasure — a large piece of cardboard, soon to be added to a wall or the ceiling of her dwelling.

MCU and MLS, *Kids playing*

Strange as it may seem, entire families are born ... marry ... have children ... then die; never leaving their Batture colonies.

Various shots of young men walking down levee; older people on porches; woman hanging washing; little girl playing with dog; men lounging on levee

And surprisingly enough these Batture People, generally, don't give the outside world too much trouble.

Most of them simply wish to be left alone; their levees and their river keeping out most intruders.

Police officers whose beat includes this particular Batture colony (just below the Corps of Engineers), report the Batture People give them very little trouble.

In fact, it is rare that a policeman is called upon to enter the Battures, except for an occasional drunk — slipping, sliding, and sleeping on a levee.

Say the police, in effect: the Batture People are often better citizens than many of the "Better Citizens."

MLS, *Negro man and white neighbor talking near walkway*

Almost all of these dwelling places are mixed — with Negro and white families living door-to-door. Though there appears to be little social mixing, there is rarely trouble either.

LS, *Little girl walking along wooden walkway;* MS *reverse to show little girl approaching church; Over the shoulder reverse shows sign on church; various shots of steeple and composition of building*	This reporter could come up with a pretty long list of things these people do *not* have.... But something they do have is their own church. Their church...except for the steeple...looks very much like any other Batture dwelling: poised on stilts, fashioned of hunks of wood, mostly driftwood from the river.
CU, *Sign on church*	Appropriately enough their church is called "The Noah's Ark Church." It really springs to life on Sundays and has its own regular preacher — a fellow Batture Dweller.
LS, *Various dwellings; Some* MCU's *indicating wires leading into houses*	Among the things these Batture Dwellers do *not* have, one must include electricity, gas, and running water. (Except, that is, where some sort of tap-in to lines and...sort of..."borrow" from the utility people.)
Various summary shots of dwellings and dwellers	Although these Batture Dwellers live in shacks and shanties, it wouldn't be quite accurate to think of them as slum-dwellers. A slum usually suggests people living in circumstances made necessary because of poverty. And though the Batture Dwellers might be poor, in many cases they appear to live on the Battures by choice; because they want to, not because they have to.
	But time and progress keep pushing the Batture colonies out of existence. While one colony is erased, however, another one will invariably spring up. Despite progress, it seems safe to say we will always have our Batture Dwellers.
LS, *Silhouette of batture dwellings, with sinking sun on river*	Almost as safe as to say, we will always have our river.

(Music: up to fill)

Feature Ideas

Keep a file on feature ideas. You can do a feature on almost anything that goes on in your city that affects a large number of people.

Do a feature on how your police department operates. (You'll be making some good contacts.) You can do a feature on the mayor's hobby...on what the fire chief does every day. Anything that interests you is a potential feature. On a slow day go to the zoo and do a feature on how one animal lives. Landmarks and monuments are good feature subjects. Maybe you've done them many times, but there is always a new angle. And every time you do a feature you've done before, you use new techniques.

About once a year we did a feature on Vulcan, the world's largest man. Sometimes the feature was about children visiting the statue in Birmingham, Alabama. Another time, how long it takes to climb the stairs to the top. The best of these was on the maintenance of Vulcan. We climbed up on the statue with the painters and photographed them as they hung from the iron man, above the city. The painters climbing over Vulcan's arms and head showed the massiveness of the statue. Another interesting shot (sure, we posed it) was a painter painting a foot-square toenail.

As you cover stories keep your eye open for feature material. File features you read in the daily newspapers and in the newsmagazines. Most features on national subjects can be done locally. For example, when the newsmagazines did a feature on the topless bathing suit, the authors interviewed local designers and models on what *they* thought about the new, drastic style.

Storyboarding the Feature

During the news year, certain features and holiday stories can be planned ahead. In shooting films of high production value, such as the feature motion picture film produced in Hollywood, almost every scene and angle is figured out before the first frame of film is exposed. This is called "storyboarding" — each shot and scene matched alongside each line of script, narration, sound, or business.

Many of the excellent public relations films produced by Howard Back, Cameraman Jim O'Donnell, Editor Ken Williams, and Tom Marker in their days at Chrysler Corporation were blocked-out and storyboarded, inch by inch.

Naturally, some things do come up which short-circuit the best pre-planning — a utility pole planted in precisely the wrong place, or a billboard obscures a road, an area is too confining for camera and crew — any number of natural and man-made obstacles. Of course, certain scenes show up which improve the flavor of a story.

In the script below, note that every scene was storyboarded and timed before cameraman and reporter left the newsroom. Except for one sequence — the black-coffee scene in an all-night diner. This was something they "grabbed" and added to the finished version.

As you look over the script, note how picture and paragraph can be preplanned and storyboarded.

Naturally, the writer and cameraman did not know that a little girl would come into the emergency room. But they could rely on their news judgment to foresee that *someone* would be sick or injured that night.

Certain shots, of course, were arranged, such as the police prowl car and the detective sequences. These arrangements are usually necessary and always

80

time-and-trouble-saving. To maintain authenticity, each of the characters in the following story was pre-selected because he or she did, in fact, face working that Christmas Eve.

VIDEO	AUDIO
Announcer:	For most of us tonight will be the happiest night of the year.
	But, for thousands of our neighbors and friends, this night will not be the happiest — only the longest.
Film	
General high angle shots of nighttime city	Many thousands of people, you see, will be spending Christmas Eve on the job — because to keep a mighty city safe, protected, well, and moving means that many will have to forego spending this special night of the year with their families.
LS, *People walking by Canal Street store windows*	
MS, *Firemen gathered around checkerboard; Xmas tree in background*	Firemen can be considered somewhat typical of this group, for the flames which destroy and kill can come this night as well as any night. So tonight, more than most, they pray their biggest battle will be with a checkerboard — not a general alarm.
ECU, *Faces of firemen smiling at game*	
CU, *Side-lighted dramatic shot of checkerboard, as move is made*	
Pan from lighted tree to clock, reading 10 minutes before 12	And tonight . . . Christmas Eve . . . the minutes drag by as if the hands were dipped in glue.
Head-on shot of trolley bearing down on camera, then sideangle as lighted windows blur by	And on this holiday night, many will have to travel. This means work for bus and street car drivers, cab drivers, pilots, airline people, truckers, and the men who sail the ships or guide the barges.
LS, *from across the street, shows pharmacist inside well-lighted drug store*	This night, too, will be a night when people will get sick.
	Illness does not read a calendar. For this reason many pharmacists will miss Christmas Eve at home, as they prepare the prescriptions and potions that will lessen the hurt, the pain, and the fear of someone who . . . this night . . . is sick.
CU, *Inside store, pharmacist*	
ECU, *hands and mixture of prescription*	
LS, *Row of long distance operators*	Christmas Eve is a night that punctuates just how important in our lives today is the thing we call "communications."

MCU, *Operator talking into headphone*	Long distance phone operators this night will get more business than usual, as thousands and thousands of voices will span millions and millions of miles to carry a voice ... a sigh ... maybe even a sob, to someone who is not at the side of a loved one.
ECU, *Hands plugging-in jacks*	
ECU, *Blinking lights*	
ECU, *Fingers dialing*	
MS, *Silhouette of TV technicians, in background are flicking TV monitors of panel*	Other people in other forms of communications will man their jobs. People in radio and television, for instance.
MLS, *Newspaper city room*	And newsmen, too.
MCU, *Man looking over wire*	For even in times of rest and relaxation, this nation is a nation of people who want to remain informed.
ECU, *Hand tears off copy*	So across the city, the nation and the world ... wires will crackle tonight, carrying words, carrying voices....
ECU, *Fingers typing*	
MLS, *Inside emergency room waiting room area*	Another place that will remain aglow tonight will be the hospitals and emergency wards. Doctors, nurses, interns, and technicians tonight will be fighting their old enemies: injury, pain, sickness, disease, and death.
MCU, *Doctor in booth examining crying girl*	
CU, *Face of nurse*	Death never takes a holiday. Neither does accident or ailment. Certainly where a child is concerned, anything can happen ... almost any time.
CU, *Face of crying child*	
CU, *Face of intern*	
MS, *Interns and nurses looking over charts, et al.*	So, these medical people at the Charity Hospital emergency room will be on the job, as will be hundreds of their "colleagues in white."
MS, *Police car prowls around corner, officer in right, front probes with flashlight, obviously at night*	Of the many people who will work this night, few face a lonelier Christmas Eve than do the police officers who prowl the city. It's only a shame that this night that rings of "Peace on Earth," will also echo with the crescendo of crime and violence.
LS, *Across street, shows all-night eatery, with steamy windows and suggestions of counter-girls in white*	Not all the Christmas Eve jobs fall into what might be called the "glamour" category.
MS, *Counter-girl pouring coffee into mug*	In hundreds of restaurants, cafes, and truck stops, tonight's biggest Christmas gift to many customers will be a hot cup of coffee.

82

MS to MCU, *Girl brings coffee to counter*	Though far from glamorous, or even interesting, perhaps, this service tonight may make the difference between life and death for someone making that long, tired drive home.
ECU, *High angle, sugar into black cup, spoon stirs, spoon out, cup is lifting "into" camera*	
LS, *Men walk out onto stage for police line-up*	But perhaps the loneliest, most thankless job tonight will belong to the detectives.
MS, *Detective at podium looking over papers*	Tonight, instead of holiday cheer and the warmth of a Christmas tree at home, the detective will probably have to face the cold, ugly, and sordid details of crime and the criminal.
MS, *Various suspects*	
MCU, *Detective looks up from papers, looking over suspects*	
LS, *Line-up*	His job on any night is no picnic. But on this most special of nights, it is even grimmer; when the only cheer comes from a cold slug of coffee from a soggy, cardboard cup.
CU, *Detective drinking coffee from paper cup*	

When Features Fit

The regularly scheduled feature can draw audiences like magic. People like features, and if they know a certain news program will satisfy this appetite every day, or even every week, their tuning habits can be coaxed to your station.

But where will these features fit? After all, a feature should run as long as it takes to tell the story. And many of the best will go three minutes or more. How do you shoe-horn it into the jam-packed local news budget? Well, weekends offer the best possibility.

Why weekends? Because most stations offer some weekend newscasts, and most newsmen who must put these shows together face a tough job filling the time-slot. On Saturdays and Sundays, most of your news sources and news agencies are "out of service." City Hall is closed. So are the courthouse, the state agencies, federal news sources, business contacts, and other story sources.

Even the pace around the police beat seems to slow down on weekends — except for the customary cuttings of the parade of Saturday-night celebrants into the drunk tank. There is little regular hard news breaking and more time than usual to fill, so the weekends usually offer prime time for a prime offering.

Chapter 8

IN THE CAN AND ON THE AIR

There is, of course, much more to a news show than just gathering and filming news. In order to showcase your film most effectively you should think in terms of the entire show. You must know program schedules, the audience make-up, production, and the philosophies of the station manager and the news director.

A moving television news program is ideas in action.

Here is the sum total of the thinking, planning, training, instinct, knowledge, background, and spirit of group effort. Here is the finished product of eons of communication. Here is something which started taking shape and dimension decades before that inevitable meeting of man and camera. It was born when man felt the need to communicate with other men.

Over the air the TV news program is a form of communication. In the studio it is more than just the artistic and creative efforts of talented editor, writers, and photographers. Structurally, you might say a news program is news, sports, weather; and there's one thing more — commercials. Perhaps editorials, too.

You are concerned with the entire news show. As a photographer you can use the tips in this book to make yourself more valuable by improving not only news coverage, but also the rest of the show. Film can and should be used to illustrate sports, weather, commercials, and editorials.

It is always strangely perplexing to see a station set up a large budget for news and then not cover weather with imagination. Too often directors think a gimmick, such as a special weather board, is all that's needed.

News is a big part of the overall programming of most local stations. WTOP-TV, Washington, D. C., has one full hour of news, sports, and weather every morning. Newsmen alternate in presenting the news; they use film shot the night before, as well as film shot on the previous day. They also use stills from the wire services.

WTOP-TV has local news shows during the day, plus a full hour in the evening, followed by CBS's half-hour Cronkite show. There is a half-hour of news, sports, and weather at 11 p.m. They also broadcast numerous news shows during the weekends.

WRC-TV, Washington, D. C., produces two five-minute local news shows incorporated in the "Today" network show. The Huntley-Brinkley show is preceded by fifteen minutes of news, sports, and weather, and is followed by a half-hour program of local news.

KTLA-TV, Los Angeles independent, presents an evening show called "Newscene" each weekday evening at 5:30. News Director Stan Chambers says, "A TV audience should see the news, not be read to." He uses lots of film and a lot of human interest stories.

Stations can use film to the ultimate advantage, and the result will be a top-rated news show. But, they should shoot for excellence and interest on the rest of the show, as well.

You Can't Get There From Here

A major problem in television is transporting the exposed film from the event to the television station where it will be shown. In this complex world you can't just leave the film at the express office. If you do you'll be a day or so late. And news means "now" — otherwise we mean contemporary history.

If you have a film for a network, first tell the assignment editor what the schedules are to New York and to Newark, New Jersey. Sometimes the film will be sent to Washington, or another city, for transmission on the network. However, it is preferable to have the film in New York. The assignment editor will make that decision. The assignment desk will want the flight number, what time the flight will arrive, and the shipping waybill number. Always.

Always carry a pad of Air Express forms with you. You can fill out the slips and deliver the film to the airport, thus saving time. The networks will want the film marked, "Hold At Airport. Will Pick Up." They will have a messenger waiting for the film. The ordinary delivery truck, of course, has many stops to make.

Leave the Driving to Us

When sending film a short distance, you often will want to use the bus or train. Buses run frequently to most large towns. Take the film to the station, and explain to the shipping agent how important it is that the film arrive on time. He will usually cooperate. When you can't make the trip to the airport or the bus station, have a taxi take the film. All packages should be marked with the phone number of the addressee and "Call on Arrival." By learning the techniques of shipping you will get more films to the station and on the air.

Reporting

Often the cameraman will have to be the reporter too. Even in those news operations where the photographer generally works with a reporter-interviewer, there will come times when the man-behind-the-camera is going to have to grab the mike and become the man asking the questions. For example, in a fast-breaking story, when the reporter is off somewhere digging up facts or people, the cameraman may find himself face-to-face with the subject: a disaster victim, the parent of an injured child, the busy fire captain, the plane crash survivor, or whatever. When cameraman turns questioner, there are two basic questions he should ask. Commit these two questions to mind, and you can cope professionally with about 90 per cent of all news situations:

    1. "What happened?"

    2. "What did you think when ....?"

WBRC-TV News Director Harry Mabry says to avoid asking questions that can be answered with a simple yes or no. In fact, in an age when too many interviewers seem to talk on and on, upstaging the news subject, it might be refreshing to confine these verbose characters to the two above questions.

Remember:

"What happened?"

"What did you think when ....?"

The "Poop Sheet"

This is the information furnished by the cameraman. From it, the editor-writer team pieces together the words and pictures that make or break the story. A good poop sheet can, in fact, be an entire envelope of material — ranging from the cameraman's shot list all the way to printed programs, newspaper clippings, and hand-outs.

Many news departments furnish their cameraman with their own version of an information sheet. The cameraman can thus write in the appropriate blank spaces:

    a. Nature of story (flood, robbery, election, etc.);

    b. Type of film used (daylight or fast);

    c. Special processing instructions ("Force the hell out of this. I shot wide open but the light was miserable.");

    d. Other technical information as requested by the particular newsroom.

The shot sequence sheet might look like this.

SCENE ORDER	APPROX. LENGTH	SCENE
1.	10 secs.	Establishing shot City Hall
2.	5 secs.	Sign on Door "Council in Session"
3.	5 secs.	MS, crowd

4.	5 secs.	LS, of same
5.	10 secs.	City Manager Phelps reading complaint of suburbanites protesting once-a-week garbage pick-up
6.	10 secs.	MS, A. J. Abernathy, spokesman for suburban group
7.	5 secs.	CU, same
8.	5 secs.	Over-the-shoulder showing back of Abernathy and City Council in background
9.	3 secs.	Spectators (most of them suburbanites) shaking heads in agreement with Abernathy
10	5 secs.	Abernathy finishes and sits down
11.	10 secs.	Councilman J. D. Williams supporting the group
12.	5 secs.	CU, Williams
13.	5 secs.	LS, crowd applauding Williams
14.	5 secs.	Councilman L. R. Riggs saying budget can't support twice-a-week collection
15.	5 secs.	Other councilmen listening
16.	5 secs.	LS, suburbanites look angry
17.	10 secs.	Riggs points to map — showing distance from city garage to suburb, then to city incinerator
18.	8 secs.	City Manager Phelps ending discussion. He tables action, saying further study is needed
19.	3 secs.	CU, same, and thanking visitors
20.	5 secs.	Suburbanites file out, looking less than satisfied.

Now, most news directors and their staffs would erect an altar and burn incense to the cameraman who consistently provides a poop sheet of this sort.

Some news departments, however, require even more. For example, some want exact footage counts on all scenes.

In our thinking, a cameraman can get over-burdened with paperwork. Never miss an important scene for the sake of an impressive poop sheet, but always include as many newspaper clippings, programs, and as much background material as possible.

NOTE:

As a cameraman, your first responsibility is to shoot the story. Your second most important function is to get the film to the newsroom — whether it be cross-town by car or cab; or cross-country by plane or bus.

A good information sheet is vital. But not as vital as having your newsfilm reach the newsroom in time for the next show. Once the film is on its way, telephone your information into the newsroom.

The world's best poop sheet is worthless if the film fails to get on the air!

Writing

David Brinkley says, "The news should be presented in simply stated, conversational language that gives people the chance to understand it the first time.

"In a newspaper they can go back and read something again if they don't understand a point," he says. "In broadcasting they can't. In a newspaper you put the important facts at the top and then explain them. In broadcasting you sometimes have to ease into the facts so that everyone will understand what you're talking about."

Colorful Writing

Exciting writing — it's all in the way you think. It would be easy to write: "Today one of Joe Banana's sons was jailed for contempt." But WNEW, New York City, News Director Jerry Graham believes that news writing should be colorful and exciting. Here's how WNEW said it: "A Federal judge put the squeeze on one of the Bananas today."

The Writer's Function

One important aspect of television newsfilm writing is knowing when to be quiet. "With the proper use of film, we can draw people from their living rooms into the event itself," says Patrick Trese, writer for NBC News. "This is where the writer's function becomes very important. In an impact story, a story of involvement, the main function of the writer is to be quiet. This is a difficult thing for a writer to do."

He adds that writing is learned by sitting down for long periods of time at a typewriter, and that film editors can teach you much about writing. Speaking at the Newsfilm Standards Conference (joint project of RTNDA and Time-Life Broadcast, Inc.), Trese stated that the writer can also come up with essays which improve a film. He explained:

"We had some splendid footage flown in to us from Cyprus. It showed British soldiers all over the island. There happened to be no significant story about British soldiers on Cyprus that day; but the picture was so good, we started thinking of ways to use it. What we came up with was an essay on the British presence in Cyprus, why they were there, and what they might be called upon to do in the future. But it was written from the point of view of the ordinary soldier standing guard on that island."

You can do this on a local level. Be on the lookout for good film that will make a sidebar story.

Cliché Copy

If you listen to numerous newscasts you'll find that many sound alike. The problem is that too many newsmen write with a mind full of clichés, and the news departments are not originating stories. Good writing, like good film, is simply interesting. On serious stories, tell what happens, but use your own style.

The Associated Press used a computer to find out which hackneyed words and phrases were most used in Journalese. The Univac 1105 sifted through 370,000 words of copy and came up with the following words, which you should try to use as infrequently as possible.

The word used more than all the rest was "hail." Mayors "hailed," civic leaders "hailed," police "hailed," everybody "hailed." Second most used word or phrase was "violence flared." Others on the list were: "flatly denied," "racially troubled," "voters marched to the polls," "jampacked," "usually reliable sources," "kickoff," "limped into port," "gutted by fire," "strife-torn," and "in the wake of." There must be some new words and phrases to replace these, or at least give them a well-deserved rest.

Any "reliable source" will tell you with "guarded optimism" that you should keep your copy cliché-clean.

Use facts and say what you have to say simply. If you can, and if you have time, spice your copy up, but it shouldn't be jampacked with words used too much — such as "jampacked."

Who Watches?

Somewhere in the practical approach to television news — what it is; what it should be — these questions must be asked:

Who watches TV news?

Who doesn't? (We must know who doesn't, in order to attract him.)

A very complicated scientific research study was made some years back in New York City by the Bureau of Applied Social Research of Columbia University. Results of this project were put together by Gary A. Steiner of the University of Chicago's Graduate School of Business. In his book, *The People Look at Television*, Mr. Steiner says that research indicates TV news is watched most by people of very high educational background and people of very low educational attainment. In other words, the vast middle-ground of the population is relatively apathetic about news programming.

"When it comes to news and public affairs," says Steiner, "the highly educated exceed the middle groups but do not match the exposure of those with the least formal schooling." In a footnote, he concludes: "We might speculate that the lowest groups depend on television for their news, the middle groups make the classical choice of print, while those at the very top supplement their print information with newscasts."

For the thinking newsman, then, the challenge is obvious. We must start appealing more to the middle educational group if we are truly to be an arm of the "mass media."

The Whole Show

You will be judged on the quality of the entire package, not just on the film you shoot. So, help the news director, producer, and weather girl to do a top-notch job. Suggest the use of film in every part of the show — news, sports, or weather. The more film, the more work, which means the more demand and recognition for you and your product.

The Weather

No other single segment directly effects as many viewers in as personal a way as does the weather. Think about this for a moment: how many news stories are intimately felt by every man, woman, and child in the audience? Only one — the weather.

About the only lives not touched first-hand by the weather are those of the shut-ins. And even the shut-ins must consider the weather, since it involves the coming and going of friends.

Here are just a few of the range of weather stories that are effective ingredients to any news show, year in and year out:

The season's first freeze. Winter's first snow. April showers. A foggy day. Spring has sprung. The warmest winter in years. We need rain. When will this rain ever stop? Does our zoo have a groundhog (and if not, would it be cheating to use the shadow of, say, a kangaroo?) Just how cool was a cucumber today?

To illustrate how a little imagination and initiative can transform an annoying ride-to-work into an attention-getting newsfilm story, let us consider this: Cameraman on his way to work; traffic jam because of a freak blanket of fog shrouding a mile-long stretch of expressway; traffic slows, then stalls, then stops altogether.

Now, the indifferent cameraman will simply sit this out. But the lensman of caliber and character (and the one who will go places) might react in a positive way.

He stops car . . . gets his loaded camera from the trunk. With light meter, he checks exposure (fogs and smogs, sunsets and sunrises are tricky) . . . he pans from the tail end of the traffic jam to the head of it, preferably from a high angle . . . he shoots the opposite lane, where cars might be creeping by . . . he establishes that many cars are going slowly or not going at all. . . . Then he starts working on the human ingredient: impatient drivers glancing at wrist watches . . . some honking horns; some stretching their legs; others tapping their feet impatiently as they stand alongside idled cars; others reading business papers, newspapers, paperbacks . . . State Trooper helplessly looking on . . . restless kids in station wagon getting more and more animated, as suburban housewife gets more and more edgy.

Now since the cameraman has given his shop the visual key, let us imagine how the reporter-writer unlocks a colorful, human story that touches the chord of empathy in just about everyone who has ever been a motorist.

VIDEO	AUDIO
Announcer:	If some 2-thousand bosses today got the identical excuse when employees ambled into work ... up to an hour late ... little wonder.
General scenes of cars lined up waiting for fog to lift *Thick fog in background* *Men glancing impatiently at wrist watches*	Chances are, all these late-for-work motorists blamed the same culprit: a freakish, thick patch of grey fog which fell like a blanket on the busy Outer Drive Expressway this morning. The Weather Bureau, later, had all sorts of scientific explanations; though these explanations hardly seemed important to the hundreds of commuting motorists — some late for appointments, others missing train and airline connections; others up to an hour late for work.
State Trooper	State Police estimate the automobile log-jam lasted about an hour — upsetting the time-tables of some three thousand motorists and passengers.
Driver looking over business papers *Driver and magazine* *Driver and paperback*	Some drivers took these stalled minutes to read business reports or magazines ... or even spicy paperbacks.
Motorist walking about *Driver tapping foot*	Others "took five" and stretched their legs ... Or impatiently tapped their feet, impatient, but helpless.
ECU, *Foot on pedal*	Some pressed futilely on gas pedals.
ECU, *Hand on horn*	Others pressed just as futilely (and more noisily) on car horns.
Kids in station wagon	Kids got restless.
Harried looking mom	Moms got nervous.
Back to announcer:	In short ... along the Outer Drive Expressway today, a good time was had by ... none.

Countless other variations on this weather story are available; that is, if the cameraman and writer can display enough imagination to translate these ingredients into human terms. Rather than simply relying on an announcer to blandly read about winter's first frigid blast, why not visualize, then film, a humanized story. It should still have the facts and the forecasts, but instead of gazing into the expressionless face of the announcer, why not a potpourri of scenes on the other of this:

People in heavy clothing, bundled against the icy winds buffeting downtown . . . those unfortunate souls caught unprepared, shivering their way home . . . drivers lined-up at service stations, waiting their turns for the anti-freeze . . . brisk business in the overcoat section of the department store . . . people checking outdoor thermometers . . . foot-stomping at the bus stops . . . suburbanites protecting plants, covering exposed pipes.

Comparable camera possibilities exist for almost every form of the weather

The cameraman must think of the entire news show, from opening to commercials. If the show isn't sponsored, use interesting public service spots, such as this still from the Veterans Administration.

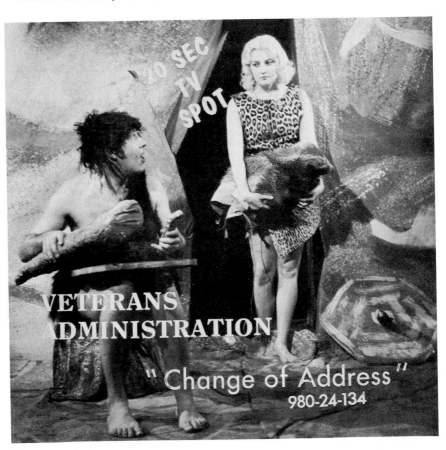

story. The trick of translating weather into the human equation is, simply, the addition of enough human elements. People doing those very routine, human things you'd expect people to do.

Some television on-the-air people are fully aware of weather's universal appeal. Many even sign-off their newscasts with a short weather outlook. In fact, co-author Willette, on his weekend news program has incorporated the weather into his goodnight signature.

After a synopsis of the weather and a preview peek at the elements-to-come, Willette signs off his program with:

"And, so, for our sponsor, ..., have a nice week: whether or not you like the weather or not."

The Commercial

When you consider the TV news show, you must also consider the commercial. Sloppily produced commercials will reflect poorly on your news shows.

If you use public service or promotion spots, use good ones. Make them interesting. Why spend money and time to produce an interesting news show and then toss in a commercial which chases away the audience?

Think of the entire fifteen minutes or half-hour and try to make the whole show interesting. Strive for excellence in every minute; commercials, opening, everything. Soon, you won't have to use public service spots.

Whenever you can, use interesting film. If you have a better visual, well, use that. Charts, maps, and stills all have their place in the well-rounded newscast.

Chapter 9

EDITING FOR IMPACT

Imagine how dull it would be if *Life* magazine ran three pages of close-up photographs of President Johnson. But *Life* does not. Its editors break up the photo story by using different shots and changes of angle. The film cameraman does the same thing when he shoots long shots, medium shots, over-the-shoulder reverses, close-ups, high angles, and the rest. The film editor then puts these sequences in their proper order — adding variety and pace for maximum impact.

In the editing process, the man at the bench welcomes change of angles, such as a side angle or a reverse. When the right scenes and editorial devices are there, the film editor's job is made easier and more rewarding; giving unity, movement, variety and impact to the finished film product. In the final analysis, however, it is up to the viewer at home to determine how well the cameraman and editor have done their jobs.

"The viewer at home should feel he is not only at the scene," says Joe Epley, cameraman at WBT-TV, Charlotte, N. C., "but right in the middle of everything. If it's a fire, the film should be shot so the viewer thinks he feels the heat searing through the TV set."

Keep the Editor in Mind

Rob Downey, of Michigan State University, as Executive Secretary of the Radio-Television News Directors Association, has had years of participation at conventions and conferences; many of which attract most of the best minds in TV news. When asked to name the one quality which distinguishes the news cameraman from the cameraman who just happens to be on a news assignment, Downey furnished this insight: "I think the most generally appreciated quality in a cameraman is the ability to recognize the story — and to plan the shooting with the editor in mind."

94

Editing often makes the difference between a good film and an award-winning film, and editing is a job that women can do in news. Here William N. Cothran, Director, News and Documentary Department, KRON-TV, San Francisco, looks over some film with editor Marie Looney.

The Film Editor

In many news shops, the film editor is also the cameraman who shot the story. In some newsrooms, however, a specialist takes the processed film, and working with a writer, cuts it.

There are two ways to edit film. One is "editing to picture." Here, the film is edited to include the best video with the obligation of matching the words left to the writer. The writer will screen the edited version, time the elements, and write to fit the film.

Commonly, though, film is "edited to script." That is, the finished script is timed, element by element, and the editor must adjust his shots and sequences to go along with the spoken word.

Incidentally, the editing table is probably the finest opportunity for the young woman who wants to get in on the film side of TV news. For reasons which should be obvious (danger, late hours, travel, to name a few) the young woman is rarely accepted into a news organization as a cameraman.

As a film editor, the woman can be on equal footing with her male colleagues; and in some ways the woman editor has certain sensitivities and feelings for order and rhythm that make her potentially a better editor than a man. If you think that cutting a film cannot be as artistically satisfying as shooting the story, then you are admitting you have not cut much film.

The news director of KRON-TV, San Francisco, Bill Cothran, puts it this way: "Only in the hands of the editor can film give the story its place and dramatic structure — its logical beginning, climax, and ending. . . ."

The Cut-Away

Without any question, the most important editing tool is also the most elemental — the cut-away. Cut-aways are short shots which are used to connect two sequences of film which otherwise could not be cut. That is, without the cut-away, the cut would produce a jump cut.

Cut-aways are everywhere. There is not a single story you will ever shoot that does not offer them. At a parade the cut-away shows spectators or the reviewing stand; at a football game, it's the cheerleaders, bench, or crowd. The cut-away allows you to show a pretty majorette in one parade scene and then cut to an army tank — without the scenes indicating the tank is going to rumble over the young lady.

Cut-aways can be used to tighten action. Let us say the cameraman has a shot of the President riding into town from the airport. The first 30-second take might carry the President from a LS, showing crowds and establishing the airport, all the way to the CU of the Chief Executive as his car approaches the camera. This entire take of 30 seconds might be monotonous. But it can be tightened this way:

Seven seconds: LS, President, crowd, and establishing . . . three seconds: cut-away CU, little girl waving flag . . . eight seconds: CU of President nearing camera. Essentially the same action was thus shaved from 30 to 18 seconds and the pace was quickened by the use of the cut-away.

There are five rules to good cut-aways:

(1) They must be in character or mood with the story (a smiling face at an accident scene would be in bad taste) ; (2) they must reveal something other than the preceding or succeeding scenes; (3) they should be varied; (4) they should be long enough — two to three seconds; (5) they should be as imaginative as possible.

The Cut-In

The cut-in is different from the cut-away in that it deliberately includes action from the preceding or succeeding shot and sometimes from both. This device can shorten scenes, provide some variety and punch, and does so without a change in the flow of movement. In effect, the cut-in is an additional shot of the same scene.

Suppose you are editing a film of a fire, and the fireman is shown chopping through a roof. Imagine the shot to be a medium one — that is, it covers him from helmet to fire boots. If the cameraman has shot a close-up of the axe biting into the roof he can cut from the medium shot to the CU (and even back again). The CU becomes the cut-in.

Bruce Palmer, News Director KWTV, Oklahoma City, and 1965 President of RTNDA, checks a newsfilm.

Hal Salor, news photographer, WTOP-TV, Washington, D. C., takes a close look at a film he is editing.

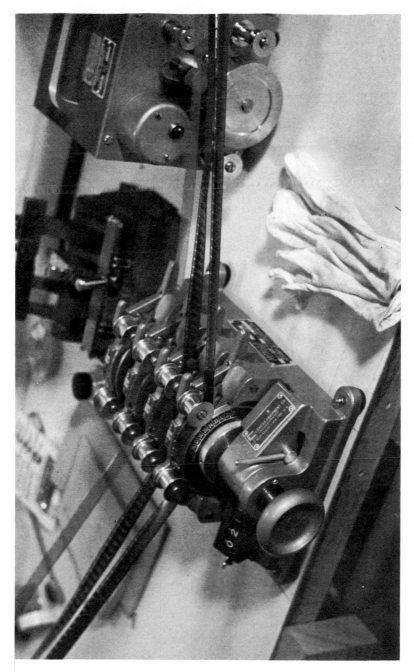

The synchronizer keeps film and sound track together or is used to synchronize A and B roll editing.

A sound reader is needed in every news department.

Editor Ken Williams of Chrysler knows the value of the photographer and editor working together. Here he's shown with a photographer on assignment.

The Match-Cut

Any two scenes which cut together smoothly with no jarring or distracting effect are match cuts. Or as the pros say, "they cut." By changing angles, matching movement, or by using cut-ins, match cuts can be woven into stories to give them a certain big production flavor, as if the story were covered by several cameramen, not just one.

In shooting a basketball game, scenes from the high balcony, behind the bench, beneath the basket, and along the baseline can usually be cut together with desirable results.

Scenes do not cut if (1) the background is out of character; (2) if a subject's expression has changed; (3) if the movement changes pace or direction; or (4) if the scenes jump or do not blend together without a cut-away or cut-in.

The Right Sequence

Ken Williams, of Chrysler Corp., has been around motion pictures for some three decades. His experience ranges from Marine combat cameraman, to service in the film production department of NBC. In the production of his many award-winning films, Williams feels that skillful editing provided the most elevating dimension. His awards include a 1948 Academy Award winner, "Symphony of a City"; a Vienna Film Festival winner in 1950 for "Uncommon Valor"; and a citation from Sylvania for his 1954 production of "The Beautiful Potomac."

"Professional film editing," he says, "is one of the most painstaking, imaginative, backbreaking arts practiced today. Just as the writer chooses the right descriptive adjective or modifying adverb, the right sentence or paragraph; the film editor must have the knowledge and instinct to choose the right long shot, the right close-up or medium shot, and instinctively know where to insert the extreme close-up for impact. Above all, he must understand life — those emotions which motivate people and cause them either to accept or reject an idea or theme."

For the TV newsfilm editor, Williams feels a certain individual style should be developed — taking into consideration his newsroom, his cameramen, and the amount of time he has for film cutting. He offers these five rules:

(1) Keep it uncluttered; (2) make sure the film tells the story; (3) use cut-aways only when they add impact, tighten up the pace or action, never just because they are available; (4) listen to criticism as well as applause; (5) keep on the good side of your cameraman.

For practice, he suggests you take an old story and recut it to see how you can improve it.

It's An Art

You can learn the mechanical operation of making a splice quicker than you could read about how to do it. In five minutes at the editing table the mechanical mosaic fits into place.

What takes years is the "spiritual" aspect of film editing. So, except for a brief description of the editing table, we have concentrated on the artistic angle — not the mechanics. Here is what you will need:

REWINDS — Get "gang" rewinds. These will accommodate cross-editing and easy accommodation of out-takes. Gang rewinds cost only a few dollars more. They will spare editors nightmares for years to come.

VIEWER — This is a matter of choice. Scan the catalogues; get advice. Just make sure it is rugged.

FILM CLEANER — Clean film with any film cleaner.

EDITING BARRELS — An editing barrel will keep your film clean and the cuts in a systematic order.

SOUND — When you edit sound you will need a sound head, an amplifier, and a speaker. Blooper tape comes into the sound editing process; we prefer it. If there is a good blooping ink, we have not yet found it.

A Final Word

You do not necessarily improve a film just by cutting. There must be a reason for each filmed ingredient. NBC Newsman Ed Newman says that one big reason for the impact of television is that it condenses the essentials of events, and this is true in the use of film as well as words. His advice is not to overwhelm the viewer with so much detail that he loses interest. "The New York Times doesn't edit very often; it compiles. . . . The New York Times needs to edit a lot more than it does," Newman says.

The New York Times doesn't use newsfilm, but the point is the same: edit for impact.

Chapter 10

TRICK SHOTS

You can do a more professional job by using every piece of knowledge that will save you time or make your job easier. There are many "tricks" which your authors have used over the years. These "tricks," or this special knowledge, can make you a better newsfilm cameraman.

The angle most local news cameramen miss is the use of the local angle tie-in.

Shoot the Local Angle

Often during the news year, certain stories of national-international character will break from which a good, effective local film can be pegged.

For example, the tragic fire at a Catholic School in Chicago sent shudders through the minds of parents and safety officials all over this nation. Many local television newsmen jumped into the local side of this tragedy; that local angle being distilled into four words: "Could it happen here?"

This was precisely the question that every thinking parent wanted to ask, concerning the school buildings in his or her community.

In Asheville, North Carolina, newsman Willette and cameraman Joe Epley met with Fire Department and School officials at one of that city's most ramshackle school buildings. There were some rather meaty SOF interviews — explanations of why this school, which was so old, decaying, and wooden, was still open.

But the most moving moments came not from the words but from the actual sounds of children changing classes — the footsteps echoing ominously on the wooden and rickety staircase.

When the community heard, the community reacted. Within weeks the school was given a final and conclusive condemnation and closing order — one

Get the different angle. Go up in a plane to shoot aerials and go under water to film the feature on swimming. Use imagination to get the best shots.

which stuck. Before the tragic lesson in Chicago would be forgotten, the people of a community a thousand miles away had made certain "it won't happen here."

Astronauts and space stay in the news, and sometime the local angle simply doesn't exist; but one enterprising newsman in a southern city got an inkling that one of a group of newly-named astronauts had a home-town angle. The future spaceman had lived in that city when he was just a youngster. Although the trail got cold a dozen times or more, the newsman persisted. Suddenly he found a lead: the astronaut's mother had moved back. He and a SOF cameraman tracked her down, informed her of the good news (she hadn't heard of his selection), then interviewed her.

It became evident even before the camera rolled that this charming lady knew very little about space. But she did know much about her boy, so the interviewer concentrated on this angle — the human side. He struck gold when he asked, "Has your boy always been interested in flying?"

"My, yes," said his proud mother. "Even when he was a boy he wanted to fly. Why he wasn't even 15, I don't believe, when he managed to get hold of an old World War II B-25 plane . . . somehow got it carted to our house . . . then assembled it in our back yard."

Incredulously the newsman asked, "You mean he put together an entire bomber in his back yard?"

"Why, yes," she replied. "Not with any bombs or guns or anything like that, of course."

"Well . . ." asked the newsman, "didn't the neighbors object to your having a bomber in the backyard?"

"Oh no . . . most of them thought it was rather interesting . . . certainly the neighbors thought it was 'different.' "

And so did the viewers. They had a personal glimpse into the human side of an astronaut. Here was the national angle and the human angle wrapped-together in one neat SOF package.

Shooting Aerials

Because of the airplane's lungings, shakiness, and vibrations, 24 frames per second simply won't do. In shooting aerials, be on the safe side and shoot at 64 fps. At 64 fps, vibrations and bounciness are reduced by two-thirds. Thus, a scene which might be too jittery to be airworthy if shot at 24 fps is salvaged. The lens must be opened two stops to accommodate the increased shutter speed. If the day is clear and the weather is non-turbulant, or if poor light makes each f/stop important, then 48 frames per second might do the trick.

In addition to the vibration and movement factors, remember that your plane is going to whiz by your target at a fairly fast speed — 80 to 120 miles an hour. This means the subject blurs by practically before the cameraman can trigger-on the target.

Many times the subject might be in an inaccessible place. (Floods, forest

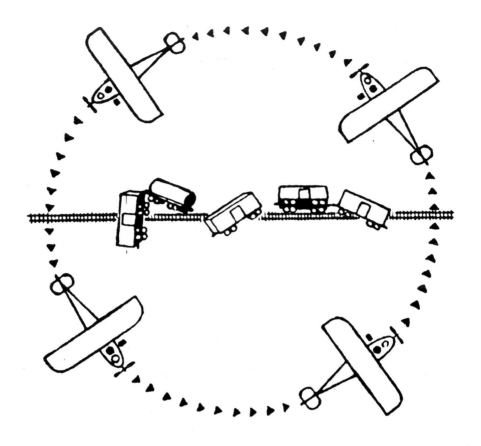

Shooting Aerials — When shooting from an airplane, have the pilot circle the target. This allows you to photograph the story without running toward it and then away from it.

fires, train wrecks, and the like all seem to have a way of doing this.) The cameraman might, then, have little more than a five-second pass at the target. When this is so it would require 12 five-second passes to fashion one minute of film — and jumpy, ill-connected film it would assuredly be, even with cutaways. But, by shooting at 64 fps, each five-second pass is stretched on film into *three times* five seconds — a total of fifteen seconds per pass.

Not only is the scene longer and more intelligible to the viewer, but the charter aircraft can start back to the newsroom that much faster. By shooting 64 fps the cameraman has:

(1) Considerably reduced shakiness and movement; (2) provided the editor with longer scenes; (3) reduced the time between shooting and getting the film on the air; and (4) given the viewer a smoother, less interrupted picture of what is going on.

One other trick in aerial camerawork: unless it is impossible, ask your pilot to circle the target area. Straight-on shots are usually worthless and side-angle film is necessarily rather blurry. By centering your subject and circling the area the cameraman gives greater clarity and continuity.

In aerials pans are acceptable to illustrate relative distances between the news event and some familiar landmark — a river, factory, expressway, or whatever.

Shooting 64 FPS

Here is an all-too non-hypothetical shooting situation: The judge in an important case has ruled against filming in the courtroom. Rather arbitrarily he has ruled even against filming in the hallways leading to his courtroom. Yet you need films of the important witness — a man who is most reluctant to be photographed.

Fortunately, there is only one entrance through which he can be brought. But the cameraman is confined to shooting outdoors. And the distance between where the man will emerge from a car and disappear into the courthouse is a mere fifteen feet. This means that in this space (and while the defendant is trotting to get out of camera range) you face the challenge of returning with something usable and long enough to be identifiable.

If, we will say, this scamper from car to courthouse would take ten seconds for the man to accomplish, let us see what happens by shooting 64 fps, rather than 24. At 24 fps this ten-second walk amounts to ten seconds of film. But shooting at 64 fps we have, in effect, stretched his exposure to 30 seconds. And 30 seconds is surely three times better as well as three times longer.

Caution: In shooting anything like this, frame the subject in such a manner as *not* to show his legs. The viewer would sense a "slow motion" effect, seeing the exaggerated, slow gait. You would be caught with your techniques showing. So concentrate on such subjects from the waist up. There are times, however, when this effect is desirable.

We're all familiar with the slow-motion effect achieved by the graceful contortions of a high-diver. This is one of the obvious uses for slow-motion (48 to 64 fps) motion picture photography. The same goes for water-skiing, the running broad-jump, and any number of other athletic events.

Here is a workable rule-of-thumb for "shooting from the hip" at various shutter speeds. Assuming that at 24 fps, the normal exposure for a given scene is $f/11$, let us examine this table:

FRAMES PER SECOND	FUNCTIONAL f/STOP	f/STOP CHANGE
24 (Normal)	11	None
64	5.6	Lens opened two full stops
48	8	Lens opened one full stop
36	Halfway between 11 and 8	Lens opened one-half stop
16	Halfway between 11 and 16	Lens closed one-half stop
12	16	Lens closed one full stop
8	22	Lens closed two full stops

Imagine you have just shot 90 feet at the City Council meeting. As you leave the building, into the bright sunlight, you wish to shoot an establishing picture of City Hall. But your fast indoor film is "too hot" for bright sunlight and the filter is not handy. By shooting at 48 frames, your establishing shot is one f/stop less "hot." By shooting at 64 fps, it is less by two f/stops.

This can be reversed, too. Let us imagine we need a shot, but the light is not sufficient. By tripoding the camera and shooting at 8 fps, two f/stops' worth of additional light enters the camera. But although the film is getting this additional illumination, your depth of field is being reduced — you can't have everything.

If only one more f/stop's worth of additional light is required for an acceptable picture, then this scene can be shot at 12 fps.

Two things to look out for: (1) Your scenes cannot have any movement that will reveal the reduced fps (resulting in "fast-motion" on the air). (2) To get a required amount of footage, takes of two to three times greater length are needed. (One second at 8 fps, when put on the air at 24 fps projector speed, will run only ⅓ of a second.)

When tripoding is possible, and where quiet shooting reduces the chance of a punch in the nose, it is remarkable how much more silent most 16mm cameras are when they are used at low speeds.

Pitfalls in the Elements

RAIN OR SNOW: A small droplet or snow flake on the lens can botch up an entire story. Check and wipe clean from time to time.

STEAM: If your camera's been in a relatively cool place, condensation will cloud up lenses should the camera be brought into a heated area. Wiping won't do any immediate good. Plan ahead on those "steamy" stories (indoor heated swim meet, a warm basketball court in the chill of winter, etc.). Arrive some 20 minutes before shooting. This will allow your lenses to adjust between the extremes.

EXTREMELY COLD WEATHER: Do not wind camera to full crank. Clean camera of most lubricants (see manufacturer's specification). Huddle camera to give it body warmth. Keep mechanism from freezing by giving the trigger a two or three second burst from time to time.

BEACH: Sand can be sudden death to the innards of your camera. Protect it and don't set the camera down.

NIGHT: Practice loading and unloading in pitch dark. It'll come in handy more times than you might suppose.

Wide-Angle Witchcraft — Of all lenses, the wide-angle can do the most tricks. The WA exaggerates shapes and sizes. By matching the cameraman's position on the top row to the picture he takes on the bottom, you can see how easily a cameraman can simulate a dolly shot. The WA makes this possible because everything is in focus.

Wide-Angle Witchcraft

Of all the lenses, the wide-angle is the most flexible. With a 10mm lens, the cameraman can step backwards two paces and, it seems, shoot the whole wide world.

Speed can be accentuated by use of a WA lens. Looking down a track with one, the boys in the 100-yard dash appear to be a thousand yards away. Then, in 11 or 12 seconds, they fill the screen in a burst of speed.

The WA exaggerates shapes and sizes. Those objects closest to the lens are distorted beyond prosaic proportions. If you don't think so, watch the next TV commercial featuring a tail-finny automobile.

A fixed-focus WA lens can save precious seconds that would otherwise be occupied in correcting for focus. With practice, a 10mm lens and an agile cameraman can simulate the Hollywood truck or dolly shot. Used correctly, the wide-angle lens can be used to exaggerate time and distance. For example, a 10mm wide-angle lens at the finish line of the 100-yard dash will make the dash look like a quarter-mile romp — at fantastic speeds. Little figures which seem a light-year away will, in 10 seconds or so, loom large as life; a good illustration of lenses being used to cheat on time.

To exaggerate distance, try this the next time the local football team has a passing whiz. Arrange a 10mm lens in such an angle behind the player so that almost all of the frame is filled with football — as the passer poses with arm cocked, football at his ear.

Now shoot at 48 fps, while a receiver cuts about 20 yards downfield. Because of the cheating characteristics of the very short focal length lens, when the ball flies it will look like it is sailing 50 or more yards downfield.

In the December, 1964, edition of *American Cinematographer*, Jay Donohue discusses how lenses can be used in an article, "How to Control Perspective."

"Photographers of industrial subjects will find this lens [the wide-angle] especially useful as a means of dramatizing a client's factory display room. Assembly lines photographed with this lens will appear 30 per cent longer, and buildings will appear generally more spacious."

The Scoop

The best way to get people to notice your talent as a cameraman, in addition to being good, is to get arrested, get beaten up, or to get a scoop. A scoop is hard to come by, because once you use it, everyone else has it, and you may get lost in the shuffle.

You get scoops through luck, and hard work, but usually by knowing a news source. Cultivate men who make news. If they trust you, they may give you that exclusive sound-on-film that they are running for governor.

Blackie Sherrod, of the Dallas Times Herald, wrote that Miss Louella Parsons invented the scoop, also known as "A Beat," or "An Exclusive." According to legend, Miss Parsons was told by a star that if she ever became pregnant, Miss Parsons would be the first to know.

The late John Lardner was amazed at this technique. He tried it on Giant Manager Leo Durocher: "Leo, do you think it will rain?"

Durocher: "Whadda you think, Buster?"

Lardner: "Well, if it does, will you be the first to tell me?"

TV stations will promote scoops they uncover. But often, they will be scoops because no one else wanted the story. Still, the legitimate beat is the top honor in journalism. If you learn to get scoops you will be on your way up. As we say, it's a little luck, a little hard work; but scoops usually come from men of power who have reason to trust you — or do you a favor. If you attempt to cultivate such trust you may be luckier than your competition.

Man Who Wasn't There

When Jack Webb's "Dragnet" series was at its peak we had to cover a story on the man who wasn't there. The story was a speech by Inspector Walter Henry Thompson of Scotland Yard. We got there on time, but the inspector didn't.

As the program chairman started worrying, we decided to start shooting the story. We started out with a shot of the clock at 8 P.M. Then we shot the chairman calling the airport to see when the plane carrying the inspector would be in. We filmed the clock every five minutes, then followed with film of the search and other activities. We shot the inspector as he finally walked in to make his talk.

The narration was done "Dragnet" style. For example: "8:55: another announcement . . . a police escort is waiting to bring the speaker in.

The ending: The inspector gave a short talk on Scotland Yard. . . . Case Closed."

Now, we got an interesting feature that was actually an improvement on the original coverage we had planned. We used one gimmick — the clock and the "Dragnet" style.

Robert M. Brennan, of CBS News, says that even if the main subject isn't there you can often save the story, and get something different and imaginative. For example, CBS assigned a photographer to film a one-man rocket operator as he leaped over tall buildings in a single bound. The cameraman shot 180 feet of the crowd and close-up reaction shots (he probably couldn't get near the rocketman, or the jumper made one quick leap too fast for much coverage). As the film was screened it was discovered that he had only a few feet of the man taking off. Brennan said he was ready to throw the film out when a writer suggested that a "what's going on here" could be cut out of the footage.

"We did it," says Brennan, "and the result was excellent."

There have been some good sound film interviews with men who refused to answer any questions. Their refusal to answer can often tell the story.

Or there was the Southern governor who answered a long question with: "That was an excellent question. I'm glad you asked it. By the way, would you repeat it again?"

The point of this is that a photographer who is really interested in getting stories gets a story even when things go wrong. But it takes imagination.

The Running Gag

In making a feature of a light story, the running gag is a great peg on which to hang your yarn.

It's the Fourth of July. Your News Department has decided to reflect the community as to "What happens in Harrisville on the Fourth." Let's look at a script and see how a chess match can be used as a running gag.

VIDEO	AUDIO
Live intro	It's hardly news . . . but today is the Fourth of July.
Film of heavy traffic action	This Fourth started off as most Fourths do . . . with heavy lines of traffic carrying the city people to the country . . . country people into the city.
LS, *chess tournament*	At the YMCA, however, the flavor of the Fourth was less feverish, as chess fanciers from all over the state met for a championship chess tournament.
MS, *chess player contemplating his move*	In chess, no one's ever in a hurry.
Scenes at swim meet	A far cry from municipal pool, where everyone was in a hurry. The 16th Annual Fourth of July Swim Meet attracted some 120 young swimmers and divers, competing in 26 events.
MS, *chess player contemplating his move*	Meanwhile, back at the chess tournament, defending champ Ralph Maxwell thinks this one out carefully . . .
Scenes, fireman's barbecue	At Fire Station Number 3, the Ladies Auxiliary prepared hundreds of pounds of barbecue for the thousands of residents who, each year on the Fourth, forsake their backyard grills for the "Professional Variety" of barbecues. The proceeds go to give a happy Christmas to youngsters confined in the State Home for the Rude.
Scenes, family picnic	Still, a great many families on the Fourth have their own private celebrations — picnics in the backyard, or at nearby picnic grounds.
MS, *chess player contemplates his move*	Meanwhile, back at the "Y," the action picks up and tension mounts to fever pitch. Will he move the rook or won't he?
Scenes, city hall flag raising	The patriotic side of the Fourth was kept kindled by local veterans, Reserve and National Guard groups at City Hall. Today marked the 42nd consecutive year that this flag has been raised. It was the same 48-star flag that was flown for the first time over Harrisville on Armistice Day. 1918, signalling the climax of the "War to End All Wars."

MS, *chess player contemplates his move*	Oh, yes ... and at the YMCA ... the chess match goes on (and on ... and on).
Scenes, evening traffic	But slowly, Fourth of July, 19____, was drawing to a close. Squalling kids and muttering parents were driving home; the city people back from the country; the country people back from the city.
Scenes, fireworks	Shortly after sunset, the Fourth ended, on a spectacular, pyrotechnic note, with a fireworks display near the airport. With the last burst of fireworks and the black of night quickly cloaking the rocket's red glare ... the Fourth of July came to an end. ...
MS, *player contemplates,* CU, *expression of discovery* CU, *hand moving chess piece,* CU, *expression of smug satisfaction*	Except, of course for the gruelling proceedings at the "Y." *(Aside, mixed by* AUDIO *with fanfare then rising cheers.)* Wait ... our chess champ may be ... yes he is ... he's actually going to make a move! The move is made and the chess match is over. *(*AUDIO: *Bring in fanfare, cheers, applause, etc.)*

The Still

While film is usually best, there are times when a still is needed for impact and drama. Sometimes a still (maybe on the rear screen) is all you need for a short story; or, because you are covering a story just before air-time, a Polaroid still can be used. When the developing machine is out of order you can use stills as features and come up with an interesting cast. Stills have been used effectively with film in documentaries. Old photos are often used in historical documentaries.

Remember, the studio camera can give movement, new angles, and close-up effects to stills. When still photos came over the wire of James J. Fahey, the 1964 Garbage Man of the Year, they were used to produce a feature. Here's how it went:

VIDEO	**AUDIO**
On pix *Close-up Fahey*	The Garbage Man of the Year, just named, is not letting success go to his head. James J. Fahey, who is the author of the well-reviewed book, *Pacific War Diary 1942–45,* was honored by the "Refuse Removal Journal" for "Outstanding Contribution to the Industry."
On pix *Fahey by garbage truck*	
On pix *Fahey driving truck*	Said a spokesman: "Jim Fahey has upgraded the garbage man."

On head shot *Fahey*	The garbage collector, who collected royalties on the story of his life as a seaman, and donated these royalties to charity, continues to live on the salary
On pix *Truck* *(from pix 2)*	he earns driving a garbage truck in Waltham, Mass. The 46-year-old bachelor said lots of people ask him why he's still a garbage man.
On close-up *Fahey* *(pix 1)*	His answer: "It's an honorable profession, and I'm happy."

The same photos can be used several times in a story. You can use close-ups of the people in the photos as well as long-shots. You can also use a series of photos in this manner, and run a tape of the subject's voice under the photos.

We All Need Advice

As a photographer, you want to win friends and photograph people. You want to help the subject (in most cases) look as good (or at least no worse) and intelligent as he or she is.

Edward T. Ryan, Director of News, WTOP-TV, Washington, D. C., says the camera has a knife-like quality, which allows it to peel away certain veneers and phony qualities. Says Ryan: "It will flick away pretense and focus on reality. Used with perceptiveness and purpose . . . the camera is one of our most powerful supports in disclosing and reporting the news."

He adds: "But anyone who has ever made this effort [to cover news] . . . knows that there are shadowed corners and curves of meaning that words can't reach. There is where the camera can look and reveal."

Take this revealing quality into consideration when filming people and advise them on how to look their best on television.

PR Films

Jim O'Donnell started out as a news cameraman in Indiana. He then joined the motion picture staff of Chrysler Corporation — in those days when Chrysler put out the best newsfilm releases in the business.

Today Jim is Managing Editor of National Television News, Detroit, one of the nation's best production outfits for public relations films. Although his product is, by nature, a soft-sell feature news item, it must stand on its own and compete as a newsfilm. It must compete in an arena where the "competition for air time gets stiffer by the minute."

O'Donnell continues: "The cameraman employed in this type of business is a little different breed from his rushing counterpart at the television station. He is an *in-between* news-production cameraman. He must take advantage of the time and pre-plan . . . for the project before he pushes the camera button.

"He must think continuity at all times. And he must have a knack for condensing the action so that it can be comfortably edited into about a minute.

He must employ 'physical' transitions to bridge gaps in action and time without the luxury of optical devices such as dissolves and wipes. *His finished product,"* says O'Donnell, *"must look like a newsfilm and have the polish of a full-fledged production."*

This final sentence is most important. It is, perhaps, the key ingredient to successfully producing a "handout" film which will be used on the local stations.

In other words, the industrial or public relations film must look good — but not so good that it looks out of place in the daily film budget.

Tommy Giles, of Montgomery, Alabama, has been successful as a public relations photographer of political figures.

"I have all the equipment . . . sound camera . . . silent cameras . . . portable equipment," Giles points out. "I can handle any situation for a politician, and that's what I sell, plus know-how, of course."

Hall of Infamy

From the campus of Michigan State University came a half-hearted suggestion from Rob Downey that we begin a "Cameraman's Hall of Infamy," or tricks not to use.

"If you plan such a hall," said Downey, "I will be happy to nominate the photographer who once went with me on an exclusive interview with the governor — and showed up with a big Auricon and a bounteous supply of double-perf film."

Willette nominates the darkroom functionary who once rewound — in the dark — a tails-out, 100-foot roll of raw stock. The reason it was tails-out was (obviously) that it had been exposed in shooting a story which fell by the wayside. The only trouble was that this very same evening Willette covered a church bombing and fired away on the ill-fated roll for CBS. After CBS processed the film the assignment desk man called Willette and confided, "I thought I had seen everything. But this is a real first — the first time I had ever seen newsfilm that was double-exposed."

A photographer we heard of in Portland, Oregon, once shot a beauty contest and forgot his parallax adjustment. It was a rare sight during the screening to watch 100 feet of bathing beauties fly by — every one headless — decapitated in every frame.

In the Ivory Tower

It is easy to look down on your city, or particular events or persons, and pass judgment. A newsman can do this. Just make sure you're right, and not judging people by how they match your personal beliefs.

Some newsmen are too quick to judge when they don't have all the facts. When you are dealing with reputations you must be sure you're right. There is no place for vindictiveness in news coverage. This is as important as anything a newsman has to learn.

Chapter 11

HUMOR

ABC Newscaster Edward P. Morgan says: "I learned from James Thurber the invaluable lesson that one of the best ways to penetrate the jungles of civilization is to go armed with the lance of sardonic humor, tracking down the ubiquitous humbug, running through the stuff-shirted wild bore, and bagging the puff-breasted piffle bird along the way."

Morgan and NBC's wry newscaster David Brinkley have led the way in bringing humor to television and radio news, proving that there is a place for humor in news. Harry Reasoner, resident wit at CBS, says: "Brinkley has made it possible for guys like me to report the news as we see it without the need of playing everything straight."

But humor is hard to find on most local television and radio news shows. Read any newspaper and you find humor columns, funny features, and comics along with the news of the murders and wars.

It was customary for some time to end news shows with a "kicker" or humorous story, usually from the wire. There are lots of funny things going on everywhere, and you can communicate to your audience that all is not death and doom by covering the lighter side of the news. Humorous stories do not have to be at the end of the broadcast, nor do they have to be from the wire. Film the humorous story, using camera tricks — slow motion, fast motion, the long lens for special effects.

Even Brinkley's solemn partner, Chet Huntley, sometimes uses humor. He was narrating a film report on the discovery of a dead whale in New York harbor; the story was: what do you do with a multi-ton dead whale? The Army had taken charge of the dead whale and stated that it would later decide how to dispose of it. All of this was on film— towing the whale, transferring it to the Army, etc. Huntley ended the clip with the explanation that the Army took the whale because they were their blubber's keeper. Good night Chet!

116

Stills and Humor

A man tried to fight a bull in the Baltimore City Zoo. Here's the way the story was handled to snare maximum audience interest:

"Joe Jones [we changed his name] jumped into a bullpen with a snorting bull at the Baltimore City Zoo. Jones was arrested and at his trial told the judge he had always wanted to be a bull fighter, and was just trying to provoke a charge. He provoked a charge, all right. The charge was disorderly conduct."

For visuals we used still photos of the bull at the zoo, of the bull fighter in court, and of the "charging" judge. The clip ended with a close-up photo of the bull and a sound-effects library "mooooooo," which had to do because we had no bull sounds. And that's no bull.

Maybe you have so many interesting hard news stories to cover in your area that you don't need to use features. If that is true you still need some humor to keep your audience from becoming pessimistic. To give a well-rounded picture of everyday life, inject some humor into your newscasts.

A Warning

But a few words of warning about humor. If you are new on the job (and want to keep it) go slow at first. Any form of creativity needs to be built up. Despite what most people would like to believe, television executives are not known for their creativity, and they have even less reputation for courage.

At the typical local television station, two phone calls and one postal card represent an "avalanche of public opinion." And 99 per cent of the incoming phone calls and letters to any station are of an "anti" nature; people almost always declare what they do *not* like.

Of course, a lot of this timidity on the part of station management can be traced directly to the FCC in Washington. When they "invited" viewers to comment about things the viewers did not like, the FCC opened a Pandora's Box. Every crackpot and zealot now has someone in Washington to whom he can correspond. The FCC knows too little about hometown conditions or the responsibilities that courageous executives in local TV are trying to maintain.

Ripples from the FCC emanate from Washington. By the time the ripples reach hometown management level, they are waves — tidal waves. All creativity is subject to suspicion, and humorous creativity is doubly suspect.

Stan Freberg is acknowledged to be something of a genius — a man who makes commercials interesting and humorous and makes them sell products. But despite Freberg's fine record, he has had a continuous battle with the non-creative set. When he submits an idea these days he uses a test. If the client likes the commercial and the agency loves it, Freberg says he knows he went wrong. "If the blood drains out of their faces, I know I'm on the right track. That means it's original," he says.

Humor vs. Comedy

Never, never confuse humor with comedy. If it is strained, contrived, based on an "inside" premise, or is obviously in pursuit of the loud laugh, rather than the simple smile or chuckle, then it is comedy — not humor. And when comedy falls flat on a TV news program, your reputation faces a long, uphill climb just to get back to where it started.

The future of humor in broadcast news has never been brighter. More and more of the truly creative executives are realizing this. Certainly the Vice President of NBC News, Julian Goodman, was one of the earliest to strike a blow for humor. Goodman puts it this way: "A successful correspondent should have a sense of humor. Too much of the world takes itself seriously — an understandable condition when one considers the public's steady diet of words such as 'multi-megaton,' or 'Civil Rights,' 'war,' 'famine,' and 'ideology.'

"We like to think it is a mark of distinction here at NBC News that we are impatient with sham and pomposity, at a time when radio and television news seems in danger of brooding down in a slough of despond."

There is an anonymous saying that goes: There are three things in life which are real: God, human folly, and laughter. The first two are beyond our compensation, so we must do what we can with the third.

Chapter 12

FILMING THE DOCUMENTARY

The documentary is television's finest hour. It combines the best of the arts of filming, production, and writing with journalism; and although many stations are not aware of it, the provocative local documentary can compete effectively with the old movie and the network show. Just as local news sells newspapers, local documentaries capture the audience.

Leave Town

One of the first professionally produced documentaries filmed by a local station was the WTVJ, Miami, "Bumper to Bumper." In 1956 Miami was strangling in its own traffic, and as more and more cars poured into South Florida, the problem grew more acute. WTVJ launched a series of programs to point out that Miami was far behind other major cities in expressway construction and planning. News Director Ralph Renick led camera crews to New York, Detroit, Dallas, Fort Worth, Chicago, Denver, Los Angeles, San Francisco, Atlanta, and Pittsburgh. In these cities, Renick and his crew looked over expressway progress and planning. Then a trip to Washington — for talks with senators, representatives, engineers, and national traffic experts. All this wealth of material, on-location film and expert opinion, was compressed into four half-hour documentaries.

"Bumper to Bumper" hit with community impact — shaking cobwebs and lethargy and jarring Miami into action. Former governor LeRoy Collins called the programs the single most important impetus to Miami's new road system.

You learn to film documentaries by studying how other photographers film the special. In this chapter some documentary-makers will tell how they operate. But in all TV news the first thing to do is to learn to shoot film that is technically excellent. Then you must learn to make films that are interesting to the public.

War on Dullness

Jere Witter is a TV writer and producer of more documentaries than most newsmen will handle in an entire career. Witter, now with KNXT, the CBS Television outlet in Los Angeles, produced documentaries for more than nine years at KPIX in San Francisco before he came to KNXT. He now writes a weekly, half-hour documentary. He makes the following observations:

"Most TV documentaries are serious, well-filmed, well-produced, meaningful, and *dull*. Most, especially local shows, use subjects that are important, significant, unpleasant, and *dull*. Most . . . are victimized by an editorial approach that is dedicated, correct, preachy, tedious, well-sounding, predictable and *dull*.

"I am suspicious of too much sound-on-film. I think film should not be used simply because it was difficult to shoot. I repeat that I think most filmwork on most documentaries is good; it is documentaries that are bad. But mostly they are not 'shows.' They are overstated, overproduced, humorless, toneless television essays which do not compel a large audience to watch . . . or watch them through, or anticipate the next one. People do not deserve to be bored."

For the Non-Net

Documentaries are important for the typical, network-affiliated local television outlet. For the non-network station, documentaries are more than important — they are vital.

Lawrence Fraiberg is Vice President and General Manager of WNEW-TV, New York City, and formerly of WTTG, Washington, D. C. "One of the most difficult aspects of an independent station," he says, "is to gain its own identity. It is only through creating a personality via programming that [we] can achieve this identity. Through public affairs we can best reach the adult and often the 'thinking' community. And of the various public affairs programming, we find that the documentary is the most dynamic."

Beat the Nets

Dick Hance, executive producer at WGN News, Chicago, taught his bosses an important lesson: local independents can produce news shows that can compete with the networks. He has produced documentaries for WGN that have captured top ratings. His shows are reviewed by "Variety," and he has won all of the important news awards. Hance says success results from long periods of research to find subjects that have mystery and impact, and from the use of "show business techniques." In other words, he produces and films shows that entertain as well as inform.

Now the station has his documentaries sponsored before he shoots them. One year he planned six documentaries, and the station picked up sponsors before he shot the first foot of film.

He uses a sound camera and spends months, if necessary, in filming. "I don't use long, dull interviews," Hance says. "I have people talk to the camera. The camera sees what the eye would see and hears the natural sound. I create a realistic situation. I don't shoot set-ups, I record action as it happens."

Using natural light most of the time, Hance has filmed and produced documentaries in which not one word of written copy was needed. A reporter narrates the film as he shoots it, if there is no subject talking or no natural sound. Then this sound film is edited into a show format.

"I use an Auricon Cine-Voice converted for use of magnetic sound track," Hance says. "I use this small camera because I can handle it with ease. I use a wireless mike with a portable receiver; I have complete mobility. I also use a portable tape recorder to capture natural sound to add to the sound track. But it was the natural sound, such as street noises, that I didn't capture on the film track." Hance has two men helping him, the sound man and a reporter.

"I'm in show business," he says. "I have to come up with an hour of entertainment." An important tip from Hance: "I believe that I have to hit the audience in the first 30 seconds to keep them with me." His opening is thus the most important part of the show.

The first show he did was about undercover policemen who roam Chicago's streets at night as decoys. The response was so enthusiastic the station re-ran it.

Hance's "Merchant of Menace" was about narcotics. He traveled with the Chicago Police Narcotics Squad for three months, seven nights a week. He had to wait until the persons he photographed were sentenced before he could run the film.

Hance does not stick to serious subjects. When an airport in Chicago was opened to jets he told the story the hard way. He went from one Chicago airport to the other (which was opening up for jets) by traveling around the world. He used many "gimmicks" to make his films interesting. For example, during a 40-minute stop-over in Hong Kong during his round the world trip, he had 17 tailors make a suit for him.

The Overseas Assignment

When the cameraman is given an overseas assignment, he should plan to take along his own equipment — despite the excess baggage rates. One exception to this rule is Rome. When WWL-TV, New Orleans, cameraman Del Hall recently arrived in this Italian city to film a documentary, he found he could rent everything he needed. When making documentaries you must consider the station news budget and manpower. A station in a small town cannot afford to assign several men to filming a documentary.

Co-author Atkins once filmed, wrote, and produced a one-man documentary on the Cold War. He tells the story:

"The Alabama Air National Guard was called to active duty in Europe during the Berlin crisis in 1961. I decided to film this story. My theme was to show why the Alabama Guardsmen were called to active duty.

Mike O'Connor traveled all over Europe making film for documentaries.

This photograph was taken by co-author Atkins of the 1961 May Day parade in East Germany. He also filmed the parade with a movie camera and used this and similar scenes for the opening of a documentary on the Cold War.

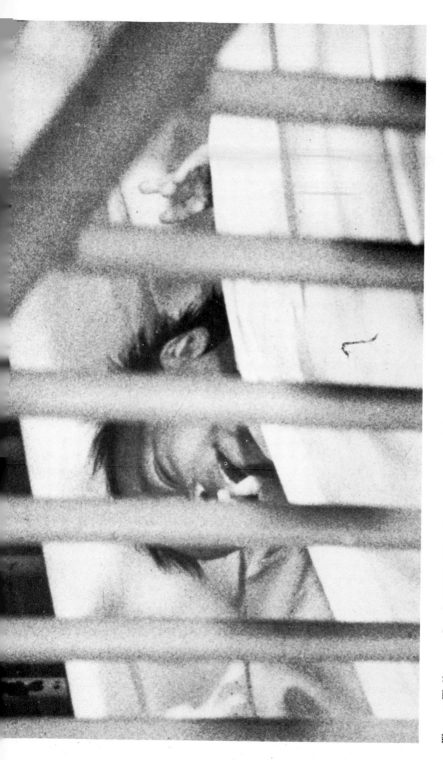

Warren Wallace produced WCBS-TV's "Superfluous People" — a study of the unwanted people in New York City. He took his cameras to the people and captured their feelings of despair by talking to them.

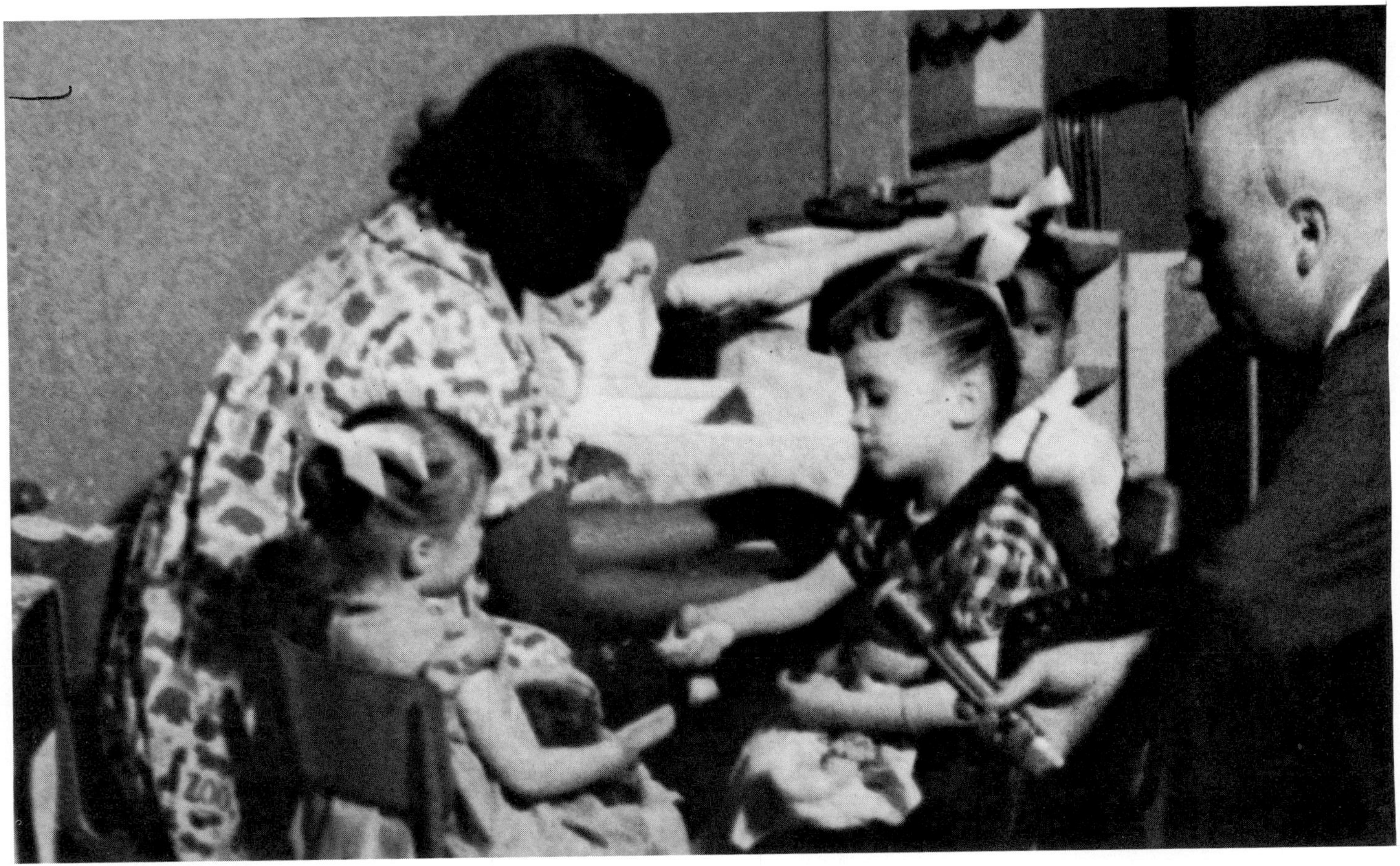

Photo courtesy of WCBS-TV News

Photo courtesy of WCBS-TV News

Whom you interview is important. An expert on poverty, Michael Harrington, was interviewed by WCBS-TV for use in a documentary on New York's forgotten people.

News Cameraman Mike O'Connor tripods his shot, which depicts where a river "is born," in filming a documentary on the life of James Joyce and the countryside that inspired his work.

"CBS Reports" Producer David Lowe is shown as he gathered information for a documentary.

"I first filmed Berlin and the Berlin Wall. On May Day, 1961, I entered East Berlin and filmed the May Day Parade there. Next, I went to the bases where the Alabama Guard was stationed. I filmed a day at the base, showing pilots being briefed, the planes leaving on a mission, the debriefing. I filmed the pilots going through their daily activities. I kept a tape recorder handy and recorded natural sound effects, as well as statements to run under the silent film.

"Back at my home base I started editing. I began with film of the May Day Parade. Then I showed the Berlin Wall, then the Guard base. I explained in the script that the Wall was a symbol of the free world and that the United States was committed to the protection of Berlin and West Germany.

"The rest of the film showed what the Guard was doing in this fight, such as flying missions, staying on alert in case of trouble."

Vest-Pocket Documentaries

What we have labeled the "vest-pocket documentary" is called other things in other areas. The University of Missouri's Rod Gelatt calls them semi-documentaries.

"Since ours is a fairly small market," he says, "we sometimes have difficulty filling a regional news program with spot newsfilm. . . . It's necessary to create news feature films . . . a unique opportunity to provide viewers with material they cannot get from other media."

Social Problems

In your city there are people who are in trouble, sometimes because of their own doing, sometimes because they are the victims of fate. WCBS-TV's Warren Wallace produced a documentary on "Superfluous People," the people the city of New York apparently doesn't want.

Narrator Bill Leonard called them "The lonely ones." He added: "New York has its share of these. We do not like to look at people who are miserable. We do not like to meet their eyes, or meet their anger."

The film went into the hospitals and orphanages and showed these superfluous people. Experts on social problems, such as Michael Harrington and Julius Horwitz, discussed the problems of welfare and poverty.

On Your Own

Michael O'Connor, a native of Ireland, is a firm believer in the free enterprise system; even to the extent of using his vacation to visit the Auld Sod to film an essay on the places and people who inspired James Joyce. O'Connor traced many of the steps of Joyce, and using Joyce's own written words, created a documentary. He plans to sell the finished product.

A Long Story

Although it hurts, Co-author Willette reluctantly admits the best, locally-produced documentary he has ever seen was not produced in his own shop — but in that of his opposition, WDSU-TV, New Orleans.

The documentary was a three-part series, "The Huey Long Story." The first hour program was biographical; the second was an investigation into the facts and fantasies of the assassination and an analysis of Long's political philosophies; and the third focused on a spontaneous and candid interview with Huey Long's son, U.S. Senator Russell B. Long, Assistant Majority Leader of the Senate.

Writer-producer Mel Leavitt said of the show: "A great deal of editing went into the final production to achieve maximum impact and to keep up pace. We tried to avoid long interview sequences by balancing narrative newsreel footage, SOF interview statements, and SOF of Huey Long himself. Also the staging of interviews was effective. The interviewee appeared to be talking to the audience.

"The final program, for the most part, was shot 'live on tape' at one session with Sen. Russell Long. Some newsreel cut-in footage was later dubbed over certain portions to illustrate specific episodes Russell cited . . . still photos from the family album were also used."

Leavitt also used many stills from the files of New Orleans photographers and interviews with people who knew Huey Long best.

The FCC

Curiously enough, an unintentional enemy of the first-class documentary seems to be the Federal Communications Commission. The FCC is not crippling locally-produced documentaries on purpose, but this Federal licensing agency places undue emphasis on bulk public service programming — not on quality.

According to the FCC, Community Public Service includes "talk, discussion, and religion." It also includes the laboriously prepared documentary. So, by FCC standards, the one-hour documentary rates the same toward license renewal as the one-hour "discussion." In other words, a station could air a one-hour talk with any local loudmouth who walked in off the street and be just as well-off at license renewal time.

Richard Gottshald, News Director, WEBC, Duluth, Minnesota, commented on a talk by FCC Chairman E. William Henry in an article in the RTNDA Bulletin. Gottshald wrote: "The FCC has made a mockery out of so-called 'public service and discussion programs.' Mr. Henry criticized broadcasters for programming 'a little religion here, a little public service there' at a conference in Cleveland. He was perfectly correct. . . . It's just what the FCC has ordered."

To compare a 30-minute, locally produced documentary with a 30-minute inane and inconsequential discussion program is a public disservice.

Chapter 13

HOW TO GET A JOB IN TV

While the only way to learn to film television news is actually to film television news, you can shorten your apprenticeship by reading and by study. You can also receive valuable training at a college, a technical broadcasting school, or a photography school. Check the phone book for addresses of schools in your area; the public library will furnish you with the addresses of schools in other localities. Of course, many of these television courses are offered in New York City.

If you decide on college, take journalism, television and radio, and as much photography as possible. It is much harder to learn to judge news than it is to learn to photograph it. You may not want to take a four-year course. New York University (1 Washington Square North, New York, N. Y.) offers some excellent courses such as: "The Television Program: Production and Direction," and several courses in film production and television photography. A year spent taking these courses and television workshops would teach you the fundamentals of television and filming techniques much faster than by trial and error. When deciding on taking courses, at either a college or at a technical school, it is wise to check the qualifications of your instructors.

However you break in, try to shoot as much film as possible. A good news cameraman can shoot film reflexively when necessary. The pro seldom thinks about winding the camera, or getting the most interesting angle. He automatically shoots the best film possible.

You must learn to criticize your own film. Compare it to that used on the networks. If there is a news photographer around with imagination, ask him to let you go with him on assignments, and see how he makes newsfilm. When learning (the never-ending process), read everything available in the fields of photography, journalism, and television.

We recommend that anyone interested in TV news read *Television News Reporting*, by CBS News, and *So You're Gonna Shoot News-Film*, by Willette.

There is no better book explaining television production than *The Television Program*, by Edward Stasheff and Rudy Bretz. Also, read *Film And The Director*, by Don Livingston. Check your local library for books on television photography and journalism. Read the biographies of newsmen and photographers.

If you don't read the magazine, *The American Cinematographer*, you aren't really interested in becoming successful in the photographic field. This magazine will keep you up-to-date on new equipment and new techniques in filming.

Another important source of information for the TV news photographer is the magazines of the professional organizations, such as, *The National Press Photographer*, put out by the National Press Photographers Association, and the *RTNDA Bulletin*, published by the Radio-Television News Directors Association. For information on RTNDA, write Rob Downey, Executive Secretary, RTNDA, c/o WKAR, East Lansing, Michigan. For NPPA information write Charles Cooper, Executive Secretary, NPPA, 114 Leon Street, Durham, N. C. Consider joining these organizations. You will make good contacts and be able to keep up with the news of TV news.

To become successful, you and your talents must be showcased. Write articles for the trade magazines and send them releases on your activities. In doing so you will help other photographers by sharing your knowledge, and you will also promote yourself, as well as your profession. When station managers and news directors read of the accomplishments of other photographers, they may decide to give added emphasis to photography in their own shops.

The Job Market

Both RTNDA and NPPA have job placement programs for members. If you want to go into television news or change jobs, you can find a listing of openings by using the job placement services of these organizations. News directors receive numerous job applications from qualified news photographers but can hire them only when there are openings. A job placement service lists these openings.

The most complete listing of TV and radio job openings is the classified section in the back of *Broadcasting* magazine. This magazine also is required reading for anyone in television. Also check the classified section in *Editor & Publisher*, although most of the jobs offered here are for newspaper reporters and photographers. As you get to know other newsmen you will also hear of job openings from them.

You have to find out who does the hiring when you enter the job market. Does the news director or the personnel manager or the station manager do the hiring? It's different at each station. Knowing this is all part of job hunting.

You will, of course, need a resumé. The form isn't important; just list your education, past jobs, awards, and what cameras you can use; describe some of the good films you've shot. Send the resumé out with a personal letter to the news director. Most will put your resumé on file, but men are hired when they go after an existing opening. Rarely does anyone "create" a job. They fill openings.

While waiting for an opening, the freelancer who is willing to work can not only make some money but can make himself indispensable, so that when the next opening comes along, he's got the job.

How? By working nights, for one thing. It is a fact that most news departments tend to thin out or simply close down altogether immediately after the evening news program.

This is not because news doesn't break after 7 P.M., it is simply that most news directors cannot spread their camera staff around the clock. Therefore they tend to put all of their team efforts into the hours between 8 A.M. and 6 P.M.

Possibly one-half of all the local news cameramen we know started this way: covering spot news events, which for reasons of the clock or calendar or geography the news department could not cover. (By calendar we mean that some news departments simply do not exist as far as weekends are concerned. This means that any story that breaks on a Sunday, which is hot enough to "stand up" until Monday evening, is yours and yours alone.)

So ask the news director when and where he is not covered. This newsman knows his own shop and his market, and he will level with you. And why not? In the long run the freelancer is going to make the news director look good. The director (or assignment man at a larger news operation) might put it to you just this straight:

"Look, our late news could use some fresh film. But remember our lab closes down about 8:30, so if you're on your way in with anything worth the overtime, call the guy on the processor so he'll hang around and soup your stuff. It'll be up to the late reporter's judgment how he'll use it — and if it's good enough.

"Then, remember we have no Sunday night show, and nobody's around here from about 6 P.M. Saturday until 8 A.M. Monday. Week nights we're usually dead on anything that happens after 6 or 7 at night.

"Now let's see . . . you live on the West Side of town, don't you? Well, since it takes our guys about 20 minutes to get through the traffic and out there, maybe we can call you if something breaks out in your neighborhood — fire, accident, that sort of thing. After you shoot, ship it in by cab. We'll try to keep in mind what hours you work so we won't drive your wife crazy with phone calls. But you'd better start preparing her for a long siege of odd-hour jingles if you plan to get into this nutty business."

As a freelancer, learn to fill the news department's needs. If they are weak on features and you have an eye for this sort of thing, tend to specialize in the offbeat. If the news department does a poor job covering a certain section of town, get a police radio in your car and try to cover that area.

Your major pieces of equipment are a camera, portable light, plenty of film, and a police radio. The qualities that will get you the job are imagination, enterprise, a good concept of what is news, good work habits, and a subtle but convincing campaign that lets the news department know it can't do without your services any longer.

A word about applying for a position at the networks: they receive so many applications and tapes from job applicants they don't even read or listen to them all. If you can't get a personal interview with a man high in network news, you are usually wasting your time.

A Newsman is . . .

The difference between a good TV news photographer and a bad one is not only talent. The good one has what we call "the eye." He sees angles other less imaginative lensmen miss. He has a desire for excellence and will harshly criticize his own films. He is not a critic of the films or talents of others because he is too interested in his own work. He wants to be the best, and he wants ultimately to work for the networks, or with the top documentary producers.

Most importantly, he wants to cover news. He is the man who lives to chase fire engines and who hungers to be where news is being made. He thinks news and is driven by a desire to beat the competition.

Here's an example of thinking news. Isaac Gershman, formerly General Manager of the City News Bureau of Chicago, sent reporter Walter Trohan (now *Chicago Tribune* Chief Washington Correspondent) to the scene of the Valentine's Day Massacre on February 14, 1929. When Trohan called Gershman to say the police were now counting the hoods' tangled legs to find out how many got theirs, Gershman is said to have replied: "For God's sake, don't count feet, count heads!"

Chances are you won't be covering Chicago gangland murders, but if you have a real desire to cover news you'll always do what is necessary to get the story.

There are three types of news photographers working in most news departments.

The *straight photographer* in the larger departments shoots film only. A reporter usually goes with him to set up the story. Still, the cameraman must know news as well as photographic techniques.

The *reporter-photographer* is the workhorse of most TV news operations. This is a man trained in both news and photography. He covers the story, supplying the facts and even writing the copy, as well as shooting the film. He may even have to call in a beeper report for radio.

The *writer-photographer*, who works in the newsroom, is a writer but can also go out on photographic assignments.

The smaller the news operation, the more you'll be called on to do. In fact, you can often learn more about television news in a small operation. Only one cameraman shot that award-winning film you see on the networks. But editors, assignment men, writers, producers, commentators — all had something to do with the film before it went on the air. Still it was one man who pointed a camera at the subject to get the film. If you want to shoot good creative newsfilm, you can do it while working on a small station.

How to Get into TV

Atkins tells how he got into television news:

"When I went to work as a journalist I walked into the *Birmingham News* and told the city editor I wanted to become a reporter. He wasn't interested. I went next door to the *Birminghom Post-Herald* and was hired to work as a helper in the photo lab.

"To supplement my income, I bought a 16mm Keystone camera for $50 and began free-lancing to television stations. One of the first films I shot — of a community destroyed by a tornado — was used by Movietone News.

"I also shot films for WSFA-TV, Montgomery, Alabama. The man who hired me was the News Director, Frank McGee. McGee is now one of the top newsmen at NBC. He came to the notice of NBC while he was covering the Montgomery Bus Boycott led by the Rev. Dr. Martin Luther King, Jr.

"I was soon making the networks. The manager of a local television station saw a film from Birmingham on NBC, found out that I had taken it, and hired me on the spot."

Co-author Willette got into television news because of training in both television and news. In college, Willette majored in radio and television arts, minoring in journalism. Then, in order to get a firm foundation in basic news, he served as a reporter-feature writer for four years with the *Birmingham News*. When WBRC-TV in Birmingham decided to get into the local news business, Willette was ready: news background; broadcasting education and radio experience; and a trained voice, ready to take over the on-the-air news productions.

When Program Director M. D. Smith handed him a Bell & Howell 16mm camera, Willette, literally, didn't know which end was which. He learned motion picture techniques by making all the mistakes — too much panning, shakiness, scenes shot too long, scenes shot too short. Because he had to learn fast for job survival, he tried never to make the same mistake twice.

Beginner's luck, perhaps, but Willette won his Sylvania Award on the very first documentary he ever filmed and produced. He was one of those one-man news departments: making contacts, covering the police and city hall beats, filming 90 per cent of the newsfilm, scripting, editing the film, narrating, shooting sports, dreaming-up television features, handling the occasional art assignments, researching, filing, backgrounding, morguing of film (such as it was), and occasionally making talks to civic groups. As Willette phrases it today: "I get exhausted just thinking about all the work and responsibility in those early days. I could never do it again. Not for a thousand dollars a week."

Station Manager J. Robert Kerns was realistic enough, however, not to overburden his "news department" with too many news programs. He asked for just one good show a day, five days a week.

Since Willette was considered virtually the "father of TV news" in that market, there was a limit as to how much he could learn. After all, there wasn't anybody from whom to copy. That is why his year with the motion picture department of Chrysler Corporation was his most valuable. There in Detroit, the widely-respected men in Chrysler's motion picture group (Howard Back, Tom Marker, Ken Willlams, Jim O'Donnell, and Bob Thaw) patiently explained that those instinctive, sometimes primitive, techniques Willette used in TV newsfilm actually had their own names: cutaway, reverse, false-reverse, running shot — to name a few.

Freelancing for Fee

As mentioned, Atkins learned to shoot newsfilm by freelancing. Willette was handed a camera and told to start shooting. However, both had previous experience as reporter-news photographers. Both agree that this is not the best way and recommend that you be taught by a talented TV news photographer.

Freelancing is good training. It is competitive, and if your stories and films are no good, you don't get paid. You must learn to think news and make your own assignments.

The disadvantages: If the station cuts its budget, the first to suffer is the freelancer. You may have a good working agreement with a news director, then without warning he makes a change to another station. Worst of all, a freelancer may never see a TV newsroom, much less become familiar with its operation.

To get started as a freelancer you should watch the stations that can be picked up in your area. Study their news shows to see how they use film. Then write to the news directors of the stations, tell them what equipment you have, and offer your services. If they are interested, make an appointment to meet the news director. Find out what type of newsfilm he wants from your area, how he wants the film shipped, how much he pays, how much film he will expect from your area.

If you have a film that you think the networks would use, call one of their news desks in New York. Don't call collect if they don't know you. If you have a good idea for a story they will pay for the call. If you don't you should pay for the call and charge it to experience. Also, a paid call gets through to the newsroom much quicker.

Just tell the operator that you want the assignment desk. Tell the editor who answers what the basic story is and what you have shot. If they want the film they will give you full shipping instructions.

Communicate. After all, a photographer and a newsman are basically communicators. Make it clear whether the film is being sent on speculation or if the network is definitely buying the film. Shipping of film, a major problem of news directors, is covered fully in the chapter on "In The Can and On The Air."

The authors know one freelance photographer who lives in a small town, yet has had photographs published in *Time* and films used on CBS as well as on many local stations. He was a personal friend of the police chief, the mayor, the sheriff, and the highway patrolmen who covered the area. When any of them heard of a wreck, a fire, or anything out of the ordinary, they called this photographer. Why? Because he always saw to it that they were in the films he took. He would visit them and shoot films of their children. This same photographer sent some film he shot to a governor and soon was the governor's personal photographer.

There is one problem the freelancer must always consider. Usually, he must work at another job and does not have full freedom to cover a story. Make this plain to the news directors you deal with.

And about that big story the networks want ... are you obligated to offer it first to the news director who buys films from you every week? When your authors dealt with freelancers, they always told them if the networks wanted a story, and if we didn't have time to copy it, let the nets have it. We couldn't pay 100 dollars for a film. It's worth the loss of one film to keep a good correspondent happy.

Some news directors are hard to deal with. The authors once shot a film of a Klan leader announcing that he was running for public office — from a jail cell. At the time he was behind bars charged with assault with attempt to murder. CBS wanted the story, and we sent it to them. A week later a news director we had freelanced for sent us a very sarcastic note explaining that we should try to film interviews such as the Klansman's announcement from jail. We couldn't tell him we had shot the story. Although every story we offered to him was on speculation and we were under no obligation to cover for him, he still would have expected us to offer him the story.

Of course there is the old admonition: "Don't bite the hand that feeds." If you have a good thing going with a local newsman and he is providing you with a steady and reasonable stream of checks, you may not want to risk his wrath by letting him down on the big story. After all, the networks don't pay *that* much for a newsfilm.

One way of satisfying both network and local newsmen is either to shoot twice as much film (if the subject is static, *i.e.*, a train wreck), or to carry a spare daylight spool for "splitting the roll" in your camera. You may then sell part of the total to each.

Awards

After you go to work in TV news you will want to move to the top. To do this the quality of your work must be known in TV news circles. One good way to publicize your talents (and why not be honest about it?) is by submitting entries to — and winning — television newsfilm contests.

Perhaps there was a time when, in order to win a national prize for TV filming, all that was necessary was to write the best script and shoot the best film, throw it into a cardboard container, mail it to the judges, and hope for the best. This was before "The Presentation."

Today, for any number of reasons, the contest business is too often leaving the hands of the news department and is being handled by the promotion department, management, and even advertising agencies.

Although this is generally true in national contests where the stakes are highest and the real reputations are to be made, "The Presentation" is starting to make its appearance at the local and statewide level.

Allow a personal insight. The year that co-author Willette won a Sylvania Award for a documentary (on the steel strike in Birmingham and its effect on the community), the home office of the broadcasting station for which Willette worked had an artist-promotion man fly in to make "The Presentation." The artist took the rather colorless sheets of script and the reel of kine film and went to work. It took him three days but when he was through with "The Presentation," Willette hardly recognized the old story. If you want to win contests you will have to think in terms of "The Presentation."

Awards, for all of their inequities and injustices, do have their place. They propel bright young people into the attention of their bosses — present and future. Awards give the old pro something to lean on. And awards give an organization a chance to appraise what it is doing — and not doing.

One station manager we know got quite a jolt one year when his station won only two awards, while his opposition was walking away with a basket full. In analyzing the meager few he did win, the station manager came upon a rather sobering fact: The awards his station claimed were submitted by his promotion director and an announcer. They knew something about "The Presentation."

If You Enter

If you do enter contests we would strongly urge you to enter as many contests as possible. This is one way to chart your progress and to underscore to the bosses what you do best. Here are some simple suggestions, however:

(1) Give each film or script a title as well as an entry number. This is in case a judge gets confused and writes back to the committee that he selected number 157 because the story on "Pet Mongooses" was an excellent job of photography. The committee next finds that 157 is a film on a fashion show.

(2) When entering a film, send a print and not the valuable original. For

one thing, judges are notoriously bad about losing films, and it just might be your luck that a splice breaks in the middle of a filming or your entry might get scratches. Remember, you'll want to keep your best films to show to editors at the network when you apply for that big job.

(3) The photographic magazines and the publications of NPPA and RTNDA carry full information on TV newsfilm contests. Keep your best films, with a copy of the script, in a special file, so you'll be ready when you read of an upcoming contest. And you will know when you are "coming up in the world" when they start asking you to judge. (This is heady stuff for the first few contests.)

One newsman who is frequently a judge of newsfilm is Harold Baker, News Director of WFGA-TV, in Jacksonville. He's a former president of RTNDA and a winner of scores of awards. His department won the "Newsfilm Station of the Year" award. Baker admits that judges don't always reward the best. But he adds: "Although I don't always agree with the results, I like film competition. Our guys, for instance, have taken extreme pride in their film-work — whether it's a potential award-winning assignment or the day's luncheon club story. Any man who comes in with a jump-cut gets a lot of good-natured ribbing; soft focus brings a chorus of jibes, and . . . well, it keeps them on their toes."

Chapter 14

NON-PHOTOGRAPHIC PROBLEMS

In this book we discuss the varied subjects and events that come up in the TV news cameraman's day. As we pointed out, many problems a television news cameraman must face have nothing to do with film, or cameras, or exposure; yet the cameraman must have the background to deal with these problems, just as he must know what to do when his camera jams.

Controversy

Mention the word "controversy" and you will frighten too many television station managers and even some news directors. Management has, in many cases, one rule about dealing with controversy: don't. Of course, news is everything that happens, and if you cover what happens, much of it must necessarily be controversial.

You would not want to give the U. S. Nazi Party a half-hour show each week, but you may wish to cover a meeting of the "Committee to Burn All Books Written by J. D. Salinger." There is no such organization by this name — at present — but there are many more just as ludicrous and far-fetched. Television should provide a forum for the expression of all sane views in your community. How you feel about these reasonable views has nothing to do with news value.

The Libel Bible

Libel is an ugly word with which all news photographers must become familiar. It is a fact that some news photographers and their bosses get sued.

In the general course of news coverage you seldom have cause for real worry, but on some stories you must be cautious.

You will find most of your potential problems in coverage of crime and politics. In covering crime stories, your main troubles will be words. Some words to watch out for are: *Indictment, Confession, Guilty*. Indictment is a charge. A person who is indicted *is not guilty of any crime*. When dealing with confessions, remember that many are later denied. So to be safe, quote the *officials* and say, "Sheriff Plea said John Doe today confessed to running a nation-wide confidence ring."

Of course, if a news story is true you are usually safe. Libel laws in every state are different. To sue, the plaintiff in most cases will try to prove that a news story was untrue. You can be sued, and a judgment returned, if it can be proved that a news story was used with malicious intent.

But you want to stay out of court. Remember, anyone can sue. All it takes is an attorney with time on his hands who hopes for an out-of-court settlement. These are often contingency cases — that is, the lawyer's fee is contingent upon getting a settlement or a judgment; usually one-third to one-half. If anything, suing today is too easy and too popular. This is why court dockets are backlogged three years and more.

Unless you have an exclusive, a controversial story will be on the wire. Check your story with the wire story. This is the first step. If you have any doubts inform your station manager, and he will check with the station's attorney.

Do not injure a person's reputation. But, if a person is a public figure his reputation is of interest to the public, and his actions, good or bad, must be reported.

Use common sense. If someone threatens to sue you if you take his picture, take the film but check with an attorney before you use it.

Many people, however, *will* threaten to sue you for filming them. If they are public figures, or at a public place where news is being made, they are fair game. The courts have ruled that everyone has a right to comment on matters of public interest and concern, provided he does so fairly and with an honest purpose. This is the duty of a newsman. The Supreme Court of the United States ruled that a public official cannot recover damages for criticism of his official conduct unless he proves actual malice.

If a story is news you will have no problem. The courts have ruled that fair coverage of events which would naturally excite public interest can be reported and filmed, even though persons involved don't want publicity. Just use good judgment and good taste at all times.

Read "The Dangers of Libel," which you can order from the Traffic Department, Associated Press, 50 Rockefeller Plaza, New York 20, N. Y., for 25 cents. It could be the best money you ever spent.

Politics and the FCC

There are many experts in every station who have heard something about how the FCC is monitoring all political broadcasts to make sure that every politician receives equal time.

In covering politics you have only to be sure that you cover it fairly, and you will have no trouble. If one candidate has a statement that is worth news time, run it. The politicians who make news make the newscasts. Here is Section 315 (a) of the Communications Act:

> If any licensee shall permit any person who is a legally qualified candidate for any public office to use a broadcasting station, he shall afford equal opportunities to all other such candidates for that office in the use of such broadcasting station: provided, that such licensee shall have no power of censorship over the material broadcast under the provisions of this section. No obligation is hereby imposed upon any licensee to allow the use of its station by any such candidate. Appearance by a legally qualified candidate on any —
>
> (1) bona fide newscast;
>
> (2) bona fide news interview;
>
> (3) bona fide news documentary (if the appearance of the candidate is incidental to the presentation of the subject or subjects covered by the news documentary); or
>
> (4) on-the-spot coverage of bona fide news events (including but not limited to political conventions and activities incidental thereto);
>
> shall not be deemed to be use of a broadcasting station within the meaning of this subsection, and who meets the qualifications prescribed by the applicable laws to hold the office for which he is a candidate, so that he may be voted for by the electorate directly or by means of delegates or electors, and who
>
> (1) has qualified for a place on the ballot; or
>
> (2) is eligible under the applicable law to be voted for by sticker, by writing in his name on the ballot, or other method, and (i) has been duly nominated by a political party which is commonly known and regarded as such, or (ii) makes a substantial showing that he is a bona fide candidate for nomination for office, as the case may be.

End All Laws?

Robert W. Sarnoff, board chairman, NBC, has called for an end to all laws and rules restricting TV coverage of political campaigns and controversial issues. He also called for Congressional repeal of the "equal-time" provision of the Communications Act, pointing out that television is a basic part of the American press, that restrictions on any part of the press "threaten the principle underlying the vitality of all parts of the press."

Photographer Larry Lala, WWL-TV, is attacked as he covers a story in Meridian, Miss. He was not seriously hurt.

144

Canon 35

Canon 35 is the American Bar Association's edict which keeps cameras out of courtrooms in all but two states. Many attorneys and judges feel that cameras would detract from proceedings in courtrooms. However, television and still cameras have operated in the courtrooms without the judges even knowing they were turned on.

An Albany, New York, photographer, Bernie Kolenberg, was questioned in a county court about how he took photos without being seen. Following his explanation, Kolenberg said he had taken photos while on the witness stand — he distracted the court only when he admitted he had taken pictures.

We All Make Mistakes

All newsmen make mistakes. Of course, good newsmen make very few. Someday the wrong film may run, or a person may be identified incorrectly in a film. When a mistake is made, the best thing to do (if no harm is done) is to ignore it.

When a person deserves an apology, it is only right to give him one. In most cases it will be a simple case of hurt feelings, which can be cured with a simple apology by letter or even on the air.

Models and Other Subjects

When taking newsfilm, you do not need a release from the people filmed. When a young lady poses for that feature on the new bathing suit, you do not need a release. If you use the film in a commercial, you do need a release.

There have been suits filed by people who had signed releases, so, again, just use common sense and your knowledge of people. In other words, if the film does not ridicule someone or hurt someone, it can generally be used safely. You must have a person's permission to use his name or picture in connection with commercial products.

You can run into trouble while using stock or morgue footage in a documentary. Common sense is again the rule. For example, you used footage of a highway accident, and the driver of the car was recognizable. You could have used this footage with the commentary that many accidents happen on your state's highways; but if you used it when discussing the problems of careless or drunken driving, you would be in trouble.

Photo-journalism columnist Rus Arnold says that what you need is an understanding of public attitudes toward appearance on film. "The editor might do better to consult psychologists rather than lawyers," he says.

Shooting and Getting Shot At

Unfortunately, photographers are often attacked and slugged in the line of duty. The best advice is: take your film, and if there's trouble, run to safety. The object is to get film, not to prove bravery.

Practice running your camera and aiming it without looking through the view-finder. You will find this trick very useful. Keep a telephoto lens handy. In many cases you will find that you can stand atop a building across the street and get the footage without a scratch.

If you are photographing a mob scene, try to stand near a policeman. He may protect you; he may not be able to. Just his presence may cause a potential attacker to back down. If you are cornered, your attackers will probably demand only your film. Give it to them, but try to give them the unexposed part and keep the exposed film. Some photographers unload while running. They stick the film in their pockets and give the mob their cameras.

Also, practice a little "Camera Karate." Practice using your camera as a block. Let your attacker hit your camera. Let's hope you won't often need this bit of advice.

The Boss and News

A news photographer deals in reality. Your station manager deals in all the troubles which affect the station. He must keep you out of trouble or both of you may become unemployed.

Most bosses are more cautious than newsmen. First of all, they are not as familiar with the news as you are; explain to them how you cover controversial news. Let them know you have studied the libel laws of your state. When you cover a story that causes trouble, explain to your boss that you have used common sense and good taste in covering it.

You are a public relations man promoting the use of newsfilm. When you see a clip in the trade journals concerning a station's use of newsfilm coverage to build a larger audience and station prestige, pass it on to your station manager. Newsfilm coverage costs a station money; you must prove that it's worth the cost. Stations are in business to make money, not to cover news.

Your Responsibility

As a newsman you have a responsibility to the public. You are responsible for giving them fair coverage of the news. You also are responsible for the effect of that coverage. You must protect your news sources.

Men have been fired for statements they have made to the press. Responsible newsmen will keep in mind that this can happen. If trouble can be caused by a story you cover, *you* are involved. For example, a public relations man we are familiar with once released a story to the *New York Times*. When the story broke his boss was furious. The Times reporter knew this and called the PR man's boss to smooth things over. As a newsman, you should be on the alert to see that the film you get does not cause unneeded trouble.

Chapter 15

THE FUTURE

Think about this: television is in more American homes than indoor plumbing. Television can be found in airplanes and in cars. There is a small portable set you can watch as you walk. David Sarnoff, Chairman of the Board of RCA, predicts that in time there will be a vest-pocket transmitter-receiver combination that will allow people to see and speak to each other. He predicts that a decade from now a billion people will be linked by communication satellites. And the result of this might be a global culture . . . even a global language.

Dr. John W. Coltman of Westinghouse Research Laboratories predicts that we will also have 3-D television. Bob Gamble, news director of WFBM-TV, Indianapolis, says that "not only do more people look to television for their news — they seem to believe more in what they see than in what they read."

Television is now considered the most believable news source. Respected pollster Elmo Roper reports this in answer to the question: "If you get conflicting or different reports of the same news story from radio, television, the magazines, and the newspapers, which of the four versions would you be most inclined to believe?"

Roper's returns: television, 36 per cent; newspapers, 24 per cent; radio, 12 per cent; magazines, 10 per cent; and don't know, 18 per cent.

Roper also asked people where they got most of their news about what is going on. They answered:

Television, 55 per cent; newspapers, 53 per cent; radio, 29 per cent; magazines, 6 per cent; from other people, 4 per cent; and don't know, 3 per cent.

The National Association of Broadcasters says that radio and television together comprise the most pervasive means of instantaneous communication and entertainment that man has ever known. The NAB also states that radio and television possess the ability to lift men's hearts and minds and therefore offer a means of creating goodwill and understanding among all nations. Much of this could be accomplished through the use of television newsfilm.

147

Did you know that 93 per cent of this country's 58 million homes now have one or more TV sets? There are 4,600 commercial AM and FM stations, over 550 commercial television stations, three national television networks, and four national radio networks now serving today's audiences. We can draw only one conclusion from these figures. Television news will become the major source of news of people in this country.

The news programs of the future will be in 3-D color. Via satellites we will have live pick-ups from all over the world.

And where will this leave the cameraman? Certainly he will still be around. Things will be different, however. For one thing, much TV news will be shot with portable videotape devices. In the foreseeable future, however, no videotape camera will be miniaturized to the degree of the hand-held film camera. The day may come when TV newsfilm is shot on a form of 8mm film, for films will always have certain advantages over video tapes. It seems safe to say that news cameramen of the future will have to sharpen their skills as reporters — not just as aimers of cameras.

Qualifications for the job get tougher every year. David Shefrin is Director of News and Public Affairs of the ABC outlet in New York, WABC-TV. Here is what Shefrin looks for in hiring a cameraman:

"One of the most important qualities is the capability to use intelligence in conjunction with his technical skills — to cover the fast-changing situation for content as well as composition of picture."

And here is the sobering part. Says Shefrin, "Two of our staff news cameramen hold master's degrees. Perhaps a sign of the times-to-come for television news cameramen."

William Wood, associate professor at Columbia's Graduate School of Journalism, believes that if the cameraman is to rise in professional stature, the groundwork must be laid years before getting the job. "The cameraman's influence on the medium can be greater," says Professor Wood, "if he has the background eventually to rise to executive rank — bringing his camera know-how along with him. And this means a college education. It means a broad, liberal arts four years not encroached on by too many how-to-do-it courses. . . ."

Few people know both the academic and the practical side of TV journalism better than Donald E. Brown. An educator, Brown formerly taught at the University of Illinois and is now a professor at Arizona State University at Tempe, Arizona. Active in RTNDA circles, he helped Willette in the organizational stages of his RTNDA book. "Seeking a career in the highly competitive field of news broadcasting . . . without the advantages of education," says Brown, "seems to be almost as foolish a handicap as entering a 1914 Overland in the racing classic at Indianapolis. In other words, it's possible that you may get around the track without getting your neck broken, but your chances of winning the race are not good."

Michael O'Connor holds a degree in economics from Loyola University in New Orleans. Curiously, after graduation he went to work as news cameraman for his alma mater's television outlet, WWL-TV. O'Connor says his knowledge of economics helps him almost daily. He points out that many of today's important stories have a business or economics angle: the effects of a strike; your city's constant quest for new industry; the budget problems facing the city council; or what suburban growth means to the downtown, business heart of the community.

Somewhere in his career, each cameraman must develop his own, original shooting style. To an extent this can be taught. Dan Moore, who teaches photojournalism at American University in Washington, D. C. says: "I try to develop imagination in my students. But, at the same time, they must respect deadlines."

The Opening Doors

More and more each year the television cameras go where reporters go. Cameras today cover trials and state legislatures — often live. Door after sacrosanct door is opening for the television crews and cameras. Even religious and medical figures are recognizing that the somewhat awkward lights and equipment are worth the inconvenience because of the intrinsic value of television in communicating difficult thoughts and concepts. For example, cumbersome equipment and small armies of technicians made their way into the Ecumenical sessions at the Vatican, in Rome.

With the proper persuasions and a professional attitude, the camera team today routinely shoots and televises difficult surgical operations.

The law courts still present an altogether unique and challenging angle. But, as camera and sound equipment gets more and more miniaturized, those vocal opponents to television news coverage in the courts will find themselves without ammunition.

The Vice President of NBC News, Julian Goodman, takes this look into the near future: "Our film cameras must be smaller, use less light, and be less visible to the subject. Not that we want to be sly about taking pictures, but the camera is our reporter's pencil and we want it to be on an equal footing."

The same thing must apply to color coverage, as well. Goodman says: "We must be able to develop color film more rapidly and use less light . . . because I personally believe strongly that color film and tape are an important part of the future of television news — not only that it adds a new dimension but it is unnatural to be without it."

Growing Up

Television news photography is a relatively new field, and as TV news demands a larger share of air time, the role of the cameraman will grow. LeRoy Collins, former head of the National Association of Broadcasters, calls for television at all levels to speak out — editorially. As more stations enter the

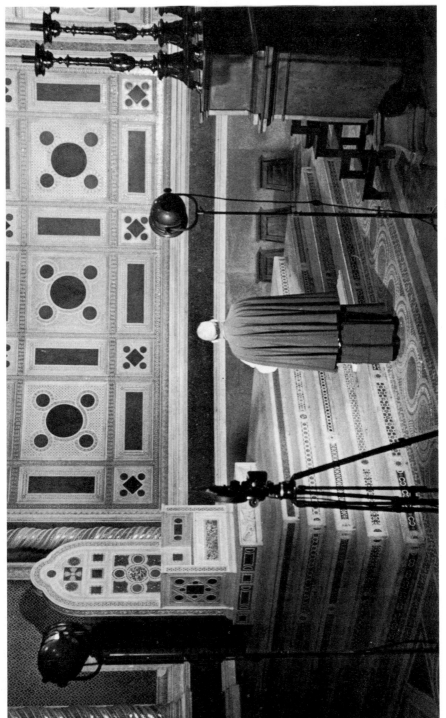

Every year the TV news cameraman gains entrance to new places. Here the camera is set up in the Vatican for filming the Ecumenical Council.

arena of editorializing, the image of the entire station will improve; this will certainly include cameramen and reporters.

Collins says: "If radio and television broadcasters are to achieve full stature, stations must begin editorializing on a widespread basis. Those stations that have delayed editorializing because their management felt inadequately prepared are to be complimented for not taking this serious step without proper preparation. However, these stations should not further delay this preparation.

"Some stations feel they cannot afford to editorialize. In the present climate, I contend they cannot afford not to editorialize."

Many stations use film to back up either a portion or all of their editorials. Ralph Renick and WTVJ have been using films for years. For some time Renick even experimented with newspaper type editorial cartoons. But in Miami, Renick found, the films were more effective. WDSU-TV in New Orleans uses cartoons and occasional film. In New York, WABC-TV uses film to illustrate its editorials, and these editorials have often prodded the public into action. In Baltimore, WMAR-TV ambitiously precedes its editorials with a 25-minute, unbiased documentary on the subject. In this way, the public learns of the subject, then gets the station's opinion of it.

Return to Reality

In the future, look for greater reality and portability. This pursuit of reality, in fact, may reintroduce certain tools of portability — like the old shoulder braces.

Joe Vadala of New York, one of the top NBC cameramen, says this steady rise of realism can be credited mainly to one documentary. "Since doing 'Comedian Backstage,' a one-hour Du Pont show," Vadala says, "the networks have resorted to brace camera and shoulder-portable sound coverage of most major events for their sound mediacy."

Investigative Reporting

In the future, too, look for a great amount of activity in the realm of investigative reporting — digging and probing into affairs that officials might prefer to see remain under the carpet.

CBS News has an investigative unit, headed by Jay McMullen. His reports have resulted in tough legislative action. McMullen's reports are filmed. He points out his advantage over the local newsman: "I can leave town after I've done my story."

This type of penetrating reporting is coming to the local station, too. WSB-TV in Atlanta has such a unit, headed by Don McClellan. "Investigative reporting is just good reporting," says McClellan. "At WSB-TV we found that many stories we wanted to cover in depth didn't warrant a documentary. So we now use three- to five-minute filmed reports in prime time." The authors think the emergence of the short "vest-pocket" documentary will be the most dramatic addition to local news programming in the immediate years.

The 300-Mile Gap

In the future we see local television news people correcting a certain professional myopia. Tom Baldwin of Michigan State University's Department of Television and Radio describes this "Gap-osis."

"In our newsfilm coverage around the country," says Baldwin, "there are gaping holes — about 300 miles in diameter. Every day the viewer in Cleveland may see what is happening in Moscow, Washington, or Cleveland — but he seldom sees anything from Cincinnati or Toledo."

As this is corrected, local news departments will add more bureaus, more stringers, and effect better systems of feeding and swapping newsfilm. It all adds up to a growing appetite for film — and cameramen.

Don't Cancel Yet

While television news is fast becoming the most important source of news for most Americans, remember that printed news will still survive. Gay Talese is considered one of the most talented and important young writers in New York today. In addition to writing for the New York Times, his articles appear frequently in *Esquire* and other polished magazines. His latest book is the best seller, *The Bridge*. Talese has little affection for television news. In fact he does not enjoy watching it. But Talese is not one of those newspapermen who believes "if we ignore it television may go away." In any discussion as to the future of TV news, these remarks by Talese give some valid and authoritative perspective.

"Television coverage," he says, "has *its* impact in sudden drama, a sense of presence; newspaper coverage gives it a more thorough and (presumably) more lasting treatment. You learn about news on TV first, perhaps; but you remember details from reading news in the press."

So let us consider this about television news: The television set is not the "newspaper record"; it is not the community outlet that is obligated to furnish the full text of the mayor's speech or the agate-type statistical and legal details. Becoming an electronic version of the newspaper of record, it seems to us, is not the destiny of television news.

Tomorrow the World

As president of the Columbia Broadcasting System, Dr. Frank Stanton must think ahead not only in terms of weeks and years — he must think of the decades to come.

In the not-too-distant future, Dr. Stanton imagines television and television news to be an international tool for good and understanding. He feels that communications satellites will truly make all of us neighbors. Says Dr. Stanton:

"There is no question that few scientific innovations since the beginning of the space age have so captivated the imaginations of millions on both sides of the Atlantic and around the world, as has the communications satellite.

"The pressing need of mankind is to advance a unity of purpose. Here, even within its present primordial dimensions, a communications satellite system can make a most valuable contribution.

"It can do this, I think, primarily on two great fronts — reporting and discussing. The strongest prop of a cynical and ruthless government or combine of governments is public ignorance. The surest guarantee of a society's aimless drifting is public indifference.

"Today, we have at hand the tools to make an unprecedented beginning in wiping out ignorance and indifference forever — if we use them intelligently and venturesomely.

"It would be criminal negligence that could haunt the human race to a bitter end . . . if we use them unwisely or fail to make the most of them."

INDEX

on film (SOF), 20*ff*., 28, 30, 38,
    39, 62*ff*., 73, 103, 110, 120, 131
on tape, 66
use of, 10, 62-63, 64
"wild," 66
Sources of news, 33*ff*.
Splicing, 27
"Split reels," 32
Sports, 84-85, 90
Steam, 109
Stills, 113, 117
Storyboard, 72, 80
Sylvania, 27
Sylvania Award, 136, 139

T
Tape, tape recording, 66-68
Technique, 11, 120, 132
    courses in, 132
Television, *passim*
Tie-in, 38-39
Time as a limiting factor, 42

Tips, 36
Trade magazines, 132-133
Trick shots, 103*ff*.
Tripods, 28

U
UPI, 30, 33

V
"Vest-pocket documentaries," 130, 152
Viewing, 16

W
Weather, broadcast of, 84-85, 90-93
Wide-angle, 109-110
Women as editors, 95
Writing for news, 88*ff*., 95, 101, 135,
    136

XYZ
Zooming, 58